BEACOMING ATTENTIVE

Embracing The ADHD Journey, To A Life Transformed

By Chris Maddocks

ISBN - 9781806543229

Photography by:

Jamie Lloyd @thejammiephotographer

Amber Wilding @wildingcreativephotography

This book is a memoir. It reflects the author's present recollections of experiences over time. Some names and characteristics have been changed, some events have been compressed, and some dialogue has been shortened.

This book contains material that may be considered offensive, controversial, or triggering to some readers. This includes, but is not limited to, themes of violence, discrimination, sexual content, and strong language. The content reflects the historical and cultural context in which it was created and may not align with contemporary values or sensibilities.

I dedicate this book to my daughter Lottie and two stepchildren, Oliver and Grace.

I've been through a lot, and I do wonder how different things could have been if I'd been diagnosed with ADHD sooner, but life has had a way of turning itself round when I did the work on myself, and if anything had been different, I wouldn't have you, Mummy, Olly or Grace. I would go through everything again ten times over if it meant getting you all over again.

I Love You All, always xxx

Table of Contents

A CHILDHOOD UNRAVELLED,
BY UNDIAGNOSED ADHD.

Let me paint you a picture. Imagine a small, excitable child charging through life like a firework let off indoors—one of those loud, unpredictable ones that bounces off the skirting boards and nearly gives grandma a heart attack. That was me. A full-blown sensory tornado in trainers, tearing through childhood with zero chill and even less impulse control. Hilarious in hindsight. Terrifying in the moment. What nobody realised at the time was that I had undiagnosed ADHD—and all the joyful, chaotic energy that came with it.

The real magic happened at my grandparents' house. That place wasn't just a home; it was a creative war zone. Picture this: a lounge carpet covered in Lego landmines, felt tip pens uncapped and rolling under the sofa, a cardboard robot half-built in one corner while an Action Man dangled from a homemade zipline made of string and absolute audacity.

My grandad was my co-pilot in all of this. A gentle giant with the soul of a child and the patience of a monk. If I could imagine it, he would help bring it to life—no questions asked. "You want to make a spaceship out of this cereal box and a Pringles tin? No problem. Grab the glue gun." He was the king of "yes."

One minute we were sketching dragons and rockets with a hundred crayons, the next we were throwing paper planes out of the upstairs window, each launch followed by dramatic commentary like we were on Top Gun. And I truly believed they might fly to another country if we folded them just right. Grandad never said no, even when the living room looked like a recycling centre after a hurricane. His eyes would light up with mine. It wasn't just play—it was magic.

And then I'd go home. Which was... different.

Cue the dramatic shift in atmosphere. The same child who had just spent the day imagining a cardboard universe would now be lying face down in the middle of Asda, limbs flailing like I was trying to swim through linoleum. We're not talking mild fussiness. I wasn't just difficult—I went full method actor. Screaming, breath-holding, theatrical flops. Shoppers would stare in horror while my mum tried to act like it was all completely normal. Which, for her, it sort of was.

Know that moment when a mum says "no" and expects her child to simply accept it like a reasonable human? Yeah, that wasn't me. "No" triggered a full internal system failure. It was like pressing the big red self-destruct button. My reaction wasn't just emotional—it was volcanic. I would genuinely hold my breath until I turned blue. Like not just "a little pale," but Smurf meets Avatar blue. I probably gave several elderly shoppers minor cardiac events.

And don't get me started on threats like "If you don't behave, I won't buy you anything." Ha! Empty words. That line had about as much impact on me as whispering to a raging bull. Once I was in meltdown mode, no promise or punishment could stop me. It was like trying to redirect a tsunami with a teaspoon.

But do you know what really set me off? Blue Smarties. Those little devils were my hyper-fuel. One or two and I'd go from "mildly energetic" to "possessed hummingbird on espresso." I'd run laps around the furniture, launch myself off sofas like an Olympic long-jumper, and laugh maniacally at absolutely nothing. My parents would watch in silent horror, wondering if the factory had made a mistake and put actual rocket fuel in the E numbers.

The energy never stopped. I couldn't sit still. I physically could not. I was like a wind-up toy that never ran out. But weirdly, at school, I was a different kid entirely. Quiet. Polite. Shy, even. I wanted to do well. I wanted the teacher to like me. It was like I knew I had to "perform" in a certain way to fit in.

What I now know is that I was masking. Keeping the chaos bottled up all day, only letting it explode when I got home—somewhere safe. Somewhere I could fall apart without fear of judgement.

Unless I was at my grandparents,' of course. There, I didn't need to mask anything. I was allowed to be me. And trust me, "me" came with full volume and no off switch.

But even back then, I wasn't just dealing with hyperactivity. I had this lovely thing called Pathological Demand Avoidance—PDA for short, but no, not the kind involving snogging behind the bike sheds. This PDA made even the simplest request feel like a personal attack. You want me to eat vegetables? Excuse me while I dismantle this entire plate and ask questions like a fussy detective. I wouldn't even eat a chicken nugget unless the batter was peeled off like some kind of weird meat banana.

Tantrums became my language. My way of saying "I'm overwhelmed" without having the words. I wasn't being naughty—I was just drowning in feelings too big for my body to hold. Nobody saw it though. Why would they? I was quiet at school, remember? It's hard to diagnose something you can't see. So, behind closed doors, I unravelled.

And in one particularly inspired act of rebellion, I faked an inability to wee—purely to get a day off school. That lie snowballed quickly. What started as a cheeky excuse turned into a full-blown hospital admission. Before I knew it, I was in a hospital bed, being told I needed surgery. All because I wanted a lie-in and maybe some toast. Karma hit me hard. And in the trousers.

Looking back, I probably put my parents through hell. But I wasn't trying to be difficult—I was just wired differently. I loved hard, played hard, and exploded emotionally when things didn't make sense. But when I loved you, I really loved you. Family was everything. I adored my mum (except for when I was temporarily possessed by rage), and I idolised my grandparents. I was a sensitive soul—well, when the devil hadn't taken temporary residence in my small, furious body.

And fun fact: I was supposed to have been born on Halloween. To make it even better, the name my Mum was going to call me was only Beelzebub himself, Damian. Yep. Not even kidding. As if the universe needed to drive the point home that this child was going to be a tiny force of nature wrapped in mischief and mystery.

But there were quieter moments, too. Like the time I was offered £50 worth of sweets to jump into the pool at a school swimming gala. Just one dive. That was all I had to do. But when the moment came, I froze. Everyone was watching. My heart pounded in my ears. And even though the promise of sugary treasure should've been enough to launch me into the deep end like a cannonball, I couldn't do it. The fear of failing in front of people outweighed my love of sweets. And that's saying something.

People always assume kids like me want to be the centre of attention. Nope. I hated it. The spotlight made me feel exposed, judged. I wasn't showing off with my tantrums—I was surviving.

School playtimes were the loneliest. There were days I'd wander around the edge of the playground like a lost extra from a sad music video. Just me, rejected by a couple of kids and suddenly convinced the entire world hated me. That gut-punch feeling? That's Rejection Sensitive Dysphoria. It's brutal. Made worse by the fact that I didn't have the tools to deal with it. So, I created my own company—an imaginary anteater. He was loyal. Fun. Always let me play his games.

And through all of it, I clung to one beautiful, obsession-level passion: killer whales. Ever since watching Free Willy, I was hooked. Mesmerised. I read books about them, watched documentaries, and memorised facts like I was training for a killer whale quiz show. I wanted to be a marine biologist. I wanted to swim beside them in open water. That dream never faded—it still burns today. My first hyperfocus. My first real love.

So, yeah. My childhood wasn't exactly calm. But it was vivid. Intense. Unfiltered. A mad cocktail of laughter, meltdowns, blue Smarties, wild dreams, and invisible anteaters. And through all of it, there was a kid just trying to make sense of a brain that worked a little differently than everyone else's.

The rest of the story? Oh, we're only just getting warmed up.

ECHOES OF GOODBYE.

The morning light filtered through my bedroom window like it always did—soft, golden, peaceful. It cast long streaks of sunlight across my room and flickered on the TV screen, bouncing off walls that had seen everything from action figures to meltdowns. But that summer, something heavier than heat hung in the air. July 2002—supposed to be all about adventure. Instead, it became the month everything changed.

I remember that day with a clarity so sharp, it still stings. I had a Scout camp coming up, and I was buzzing. Bags packed. Uniform ready. That kind of excitement that makes your whole body feel fizzy. It felt like a proper rite of passage—campfires, mates, freedom. But before we set off, my dad told me we were stopping at the hospital to visit Grandad.

No big deal, I thought. Grandad had been in and out before. I figured he was in for a check-up or maybe one of those annoying grown-up things where they tell you to rest and eat soup. I didn't realise we weren't going to a hospital. We were going to a hospice. At ten years old, that word meant nothing to me. But looking back? That word now echoes.

We drove to Clatterbridge in my dad's car, me clueless in the passenger seat, probably chatting about knots or badges or whether we'd get hot chocolate at camp. No sense of what was coming. No idea that I was walking into a goodbye.

When we got there, I noticed the difference straight away. The hospice wasn't loud like hospitals usually are. It was quiet, too clean, almost like everyone was tiptoeing around something invisible. The smell of antiseptic hit me hard, that weird mix of sterile and sadness. Machines beeped in the background, soft and slow like a heartbeat on a metronome. We made our way to Grandad's room, and my heart skipped when I saw him.

He looked smaller—like the air had been let out of him somehow. His face was thinner, skin paler, and his hands, once strong and steady from all those cardboard spaceship missions, looked fragile. But then he smiled. And God, when Grandad smiled, the whole room lit up. Even there, in that bed, surrounded by machines, he still looked at me like I was his whole world.

"Hi, Grandad," I said, voice trembling.

"Hello, old chap," he replied, his voice weak but still full of warmth. That was his thing—he could make you feel like everything was okay, even when it wasn't. I stepped closer, desperate to hug him, to wrap my arms around him the way I always had. But he gently lifted a hand and shook his head.

"No hugs, old chap. Hospitals are dirty places," he said with a grin, like he was trying to turn a heartbreaking moment into a joke. I nodded, biting back the lump in my throat. Deep down, I knew he wasn't just worried about germs—he was protecting me. From the truth. From the weight of what that moment meant.

We spent about an hour together. He told me stories, gave me advice wrapped in humour, and tried to keep things light, even though every breath looked like it cost him something. This wasn't new—he used to play football with me in the street for five minutes at a time, then collapse onto his nebuliser just to catch his breath again. But he never let it stop him. He never said no to fun. He'd rather wheeze his lungs out than miss a moment with me.

As I got ready to leave for camp, he looked me dead in the eyes. Stronger, just for a second. He straightened up and said, "See you when you come home, old chap."

I nodded, smiled, and believed him. Because why wouldn't I? I was ten. My grandad was magic. He couldn't not be there when I got back. My backpack felt light as I walked out of that room. I didn't know it was carrying the last memory I'd ever have of him.

Scout camp was everything I expected—fires, laughs, a bit of chaos. But even as I roasted marshmallows and traded stories with mates, Grandad's voice kept ringing in my ears. See you when you come home, old chap. Something felt off. Not wrong exactly, just… heavy. I couldn't place it.

Saturday night, I climbed up into a tree. No idea why. I just needed space. I sat up there looking out across the field, feeling weirdly distant from all the noise below. It was like my insides were pulling tight, like a knot I couldn't undo. "I go home tomorrow," I told myself. "Probably just excited." But deep down, a whisper told me otherwise. That gut feeling—the one you can't explain—was already mourning.

Sunday arrived and I was buzzing to get home. I had stories to tell. I'd survived two nights of midges and dodgy sausages. My dad picked me up, and on the surface, everything looked normal. But as we pulled into the driveway, something shifted. The air felt too still. The house too quiet.

I walked in and my dad was already waiting, his face different. Sad, tired, a man carrying a weight he didn't want to put on his child. He knelt down and told me the words I didn't want to hear.

Grandad was gone.

He'd passed away while I was away. And I wasn't there.

It hit me like a punch to the chest. The world tilted. I couldn't breathe. I couldn't think. My dad cried—really cried—and I remember just collapsing on my bed. My room, once a place of colour and joy, suddenly felt hollow. The posters didn't matter. The toys didn't matter. Nothing made sense.

I kept replaying it. His smile. His stories. That final moment. See you when you come home, old chap. That sentence haunted me. Why didn't I hug him? Why didn't I hold onto him just a little longer?

I had the chance to go to the chapel of rest. I could've said goodbye properly. I could've gone to his funeral. But I didn't. I couldn't. I didn't want that image to be the one that stuck. I wanted to remember him as the man who ran around the garden with me, not the man lying still in a box.

But the regret stayed. It still does.

Over the years, the pain softened but never left. It became part of me, like a scar that healed but never quite faded. I still talk to him—sometimes out loud, sometimes in my head. I tell him what's going on, what I'm proud of, what I'm scared of. I hope he hears me. I hope he's proud.

When I turned 18, I got his initials—GTM—tattooed on my forearm. A quiet tribute. A permanent mark for a permanent loss. Later, I added his portrait on the other side of the same arm. That way, no matter what I'm doing, he's always there. Always with me.

He wasn't just my grandad. He was my best friend. He taught me how to tie my laces (two bunny ears, no fancy loops—

still do it the same way), how to count, spell, and how to ride a bike without stabilisers. But more than that, he taught me how to live. How to squeeze every bit of joy out of life, no matter what. He had one and a half lungs, and he still played football with me in the street.

No one has filled that space he left behind. And they never will. That space belongs to him.

It took me years to understand that losing him didn't break me—it built me. It made me softer, stronger, more grateful. It gave me a kind of emotional radar that shaped how I love people, how I protect them, how I fear losing them. I think that's where my fear of rejection was born. That fear of being left. Because I was left. Not by choice, not by betrayal—but by the most devastating kind of goodbye.

And yet, in every moment of joy, in every big decision, I feel him. I hear him. That voice, that warmth, that unconditional love. It shaped me.

Now, 22 years later, I like the man I've become. A good man. A father. A partner. A person who still talks to the stars sometimes and quietly says, I hope I'm making you proud, Grandad.

Because you were the best. And I'll spend the rest of my life telling the world that.

THE HORMONAL ROLLERCOASTER OF HIGH SCHOOL.

Puberty didn't just knock on my door—it kicked it off the hinges and stormed in like it owned the place. And what did I get? Not a cool deep voice or a sudden six-pack, no. I got sideburns. Patchy, rebellious sideburns that sprouted like weeds and made me look like a half-baked Elvis impersonator. My face was a battlefield of acne and frustration, and my brain. A chaotic theme park that never shut down.

The mood swings were wild. One minute I was euphoric, planning out my future as a famous marine biologist, the next I was curled up in the nurse's office, a prisoner to migraines that felt like drills in my skull. She knew the signs—ashen face, far-off stare. I had a season ticket to the sick bay.

High school was an emotional paradox. I smashed it in Biology and English—two subjects where I could escape into systems or stories and forget my own mess. But PE? Drama? Those were nightmares. I felt like I was being auditioned for a part in someone else's life. I couldn't keep up, couldn't stay still, and when I failed to shine, that voice inside me whispered, You're not enough. And I believed it.

Socially, I shape-shifted. Around my group of friends who we're mostly girls—the safe ones—I could just be me. Laugh too loud, talk too fast, throw out random SpongeBob quotes. But outside that bubble, I wore masks. Funny one. Quiet one. The agreeable one. With my parents, it was a different story entirely. My temper was unpredictable, explosive even.

They got the brunt of the emotional storm I hid from everyone else.

Relationships were no less confusing. My first girlfriend was like a sister—we bonded over cartoons and chocolate milk, not passion. But as I got older, the emotional stakes got higher. I was desperate to be wanted but terrified of being exposed. I talked a big game, but when it came time to perform—to be the man I thought I had to be—my body froze. I couldn't do it. Erectile dysfunction at 15 isn’t just awkward, it's soul-crushing. She dumped me the next day, and honestly, that moment carved a crack in my self-worth that never quite sealed up. I carried that failure like a secret badge of shame, long after the embarrassment had faded.

Criticism felt like a punch to the gut. One offhand comment and I’d spiral, my brain looping it over and over like a cursed mixtape. At school, I played it cool. At home, I took it out on doors, walls, and whatever furniture was unfortunate enough to be nearby. My room looked like a scene from a bar fight—only I was the one throwing punches, and no one else was there.

And then there was the infamous McDonald’s comment. My Business Studies teacher, in all his wisdom, looked me dead in the eyes and told me I’d be flipping burgers for a living. Cheers, mate. I failed that class spectacularly. And yet, years later, I ended up working alongside his daughter as an apprentice. Bet that stung. Now I run my own business—Attentive. Guess I passed the real test after all.

There were glimmers of light too. Like her. A girl a year below me—soft-spoken but strong. When people dragged up her past and tried to humiliate her, I didn't walk away like everyone else. I stayed. Defended her. Supported her. That moment taught me something I didn't know I had, loyalty. Real, unshakeable loyalty. It was the first time I felt proud of the kind of man I could be.

Still, I didn't fit the traditional mould. My Dad lined up an apprenticeship—the same one he and my Grandad had done. It felt like a rite of passage. But all I felt was dread. I didn't want it. I wanted something different. Something more. I just didn't know what.

In hindsight, undiagnosed ADHD was the puppet master behind so much of my chaos—impulsivity, forgetfulness, rage that came from nowhere. It was like trying to live with a tornado in my chest.

And speaking of impulsivity, let me tell you about him. The boy down the road. We became fast friends—too fast. The kind of friendship that felt like petrol and matches. One day, he snuck into my back garden to rob a stash of sweets I'd hidden like a sugar-hoarding raccoon. I saw red. Grabbed a spray can I'd used to tag my BMX and graffitied his fence like some kind of low-budget Banksy. Got caught, obviously. The punishment? Repainting the whole thing and coughing up the money from the savings my grandparents had been building since I was born. Paintbrush in hand, dignity in shreds.

But I didn't learn. Weeks later, I tied fishing line across the street like a cartoon booby trap. He flew through it on his bike and ended up with a scar across his neck. He still has it. I still don't know how I didn't kill him. And the cherry on top? I once shot an air rifle out of my bedroom window because he wouldn't stop sitting outside my house, grinning at me like the Joker. The pellet missed him by inches. Hit a yogurt pot. Could've blinded him. We laugh about it now—somehow, we're still friends—but Jesus, it could've gone so differently.

Back at home, my anger turned destructive. Holes in the walls. Doors off their hinges. Picture frames smashed to pieces. Our house slowly transformed into a war zone. And every time something broke, the cost came from the same place: my future. The savings my grandparents had quietly built over the years—gone. Spent on new doors, new plaster, new beginnings that always seemed to end the same way. That little pot of love and hope got drained long before I ever had a chance to appreciate it.

And now? Now I carry the weight of that loss. Not just the money, but the meaning behind it. The trust. The love. The sacrifice. I destroyed so much before I even understood what it meant to have something worth protecting.

High school wasn't just a chapter—it was a full-blown war. A war between who I was, who I thought I had to be, and who I might've been if I'd only known what was really going on inside my brain.

THE HAZE.

The first drag of a cigarette—stolen from my mum's pack when no one was looking—hit like a freight train. My chest burned, my head spun, and I coughed like I was trying to launch a lung across the garden. But in that moment, through the sting and the dizziness, I felt something new: rebellion. A rush. Like I'd finally found a way to say, "I'm not a kid anymore." It was dumb. It was gross. And it was the hardest addiction I'd ever have to shake.

I was 16, fresh out of school with a handful of GCSEs and a place in an engineering apprenticeship—following in the footsteps of my dad and my grandad. On paper, it looked like I had it together. But inside? I was lost. Really lost. Floating through days, clinging to anything that made me feel like I belonged. I didn't know it at the time, but that chaos—the restlessness, the anxiety, the emotional swings—it was ADHD. Undiagnosed, unmanaged, and slowly taking the wheel.

Weed was the next step. I'd convinced myself it helped. The racing thoughts would quiet down, and for a little while, I wasn't trapped in my own buzzing brain. I was just... still. Calm. But the calm never lasted. The comedown always came. And soon, I wasn't using to relax—I was using to escape. I'd walk in from a session reeking of smoke, half a can of Lynx drowning in the other half of the problem, telling my mum I was "just tired." As if that explained the red eyes and spaced-out expression.

The nights got later. The lies got easier. Fake IDs, house parties, underage drinking—it all became routine. My parties became infamous. People showed up for the madness, the music, the mess. On the outside, I played the role well—life of the party, loud, fearless, up for anything. But underneath that was a kid desperate to be liked. Desperate to quiet the noise in his head. I didn't feel cool. I felt broken. But no one needed to know that.

When my parents were away on holiday, I saw it as a free pass. The rules were still there, but without them watching, it felt like I could bend them... or snap them clean in half. I had a provisional license at the time, but that didn't stop me from taking my mums car – more than once – to the garage to get cigarettes and booze. It wasn't some big thrill seeking mission. It was impulsive. It was "I want something now, so I'll just do it" without even a flicker of thought about the consequences.

The worst part? Id been drinking, too. I didn't even see the danger I was putting myself – or anyone else – in. My brain didn't do the maths. It just did the "now" One of my parents neighbours spotted me and grassed me in, and when they got back, I got in so much trouble. I obviously tried to lie, but my mum just knew it was just that, a lie. Looking back, its scary how normal it felt at the time. I wasn't trying to be reckless – I just didn't have the part of my brain switched on that says, "Maybe don't."

Then came the legal highs—specifically, mephedrone, or mkat. That night changed everything.

I was perched on my windowsill one night when my next-door neighbour, fresh from a night out, called me in for a drink. Within minutes, a bag of white powder was on the table. "It's legal," he said, like that made it okay. "You'll feel amazing." I wanted amazing. I wanted anything that wasn't the constant chaos in my head. So, I tried it.

And it worked—briefly. Euphoria. Energy. I felt invincible. But it didn't take long before the dark side kicked in. Paranoia. Panic. My heart racing like it was trying to sprint out of my chest. Still, I kept chasing that first high, convinced I could get it back. What started as occasional became regular. Then it wasn't just mkat—it was ecstasy, ketamine, coke. If it dulled the noise, I took it.

I hit rock bottom during a camping trip with mates. It was supposed to be fun - laughter around the fire, a few drinks, the usual chaos. But that night I swallowed 20 ecstasy pills. I don't know why. Boredom? Impulsiveness? Trying to prove something? I blacked out and didn't wake up for 24 hours. My parents thought I was dead.

The nickname I'd earned in school—Mad Dog—followed me through this chapter. It was part badge of honour, part curse. I leaned into it. If people expected chaos, I gave it to them. But they didn't see what was underneath. They didn't see the panic attacks, the sleepless nights, the crippling insecurity. They didn't see the quiet moments where I looked in the mirror and didn't know who I was.

At 17, I passed my driving test—four days later, I crashed the car my grandma had gifted me. I flipped it straight into a hedge, missing a solid oak tree by inches. That should've been a wake-up call. And it was… for a week or two. But with ADHD, fear fades fast. That near-death memory quickly dissolved into adrenaline nostalgia, and I was back behind the wheel chasing dopamine like it was a finish line.

The anxiety, the paranoia, the constant internal noise—they stopped being visitors. They moved in. Rent-free. Every decision I made was laced with chaos. I couldn't concentrate. I couldn't sit still. My brain needed stimulation the way lungs need oxygen. And if I didn't get it, I spiralled.

The damage followed me everywhere. Relationships suffered. I pushed people away or pulled them too close. My moods were unpredictable. I alienated family and left friends confused, even scared. I joined clubs and sports teams hoping to find "my thing," but I never felt like I fitted in. I was always performing, always pretending.

One moment that stuck with me came from my business studies teacher—he told me I'd end up working at

McDonald's. He said it with that smug, dismissive tone teachers sometimes use when they've already decided who you are. It cut deep. Funny thing is, years later I ended up working with his daughter during my apprenticeship. I don't know if he ever found out, but I like to think it ruined at least one of his dinners. Even funnier? I failed business studies and now run Attentive.

Amid all the chaos, there were glimmers of who I really was. I formed a deep bond with a girl a year below me. Which blossomed into a relationship, turning her into my high school sweetheart. She went through something rough—someone dug up her past and tried to humiliate her. Her so-called friends turned their backs, but I didn't. I stood by her. Protected her. It was instinctive. No performance. No bravado. Just genuine loyalty. That was one of the first times I realised I could be a good person, underneath it all.

But the anger still had me. The impulsiveness. The blackouts. My outbursts at home weren't just shouting matches - they were violent. Doors kicked in. Walls punched. Furniture smashed. The damage was constant, and every time, the cost fell on my parents. Or more specifically - on the savings my grandparents had quietly built up for me since the day I was born. That little pot of love, of security, was chipped away with every broken item, until there was nothing left.

By the time I was old enough to inherit it, the account was empty. Not because of emergencies. Not because of hard times. But because I'd destroyed it - literally.

I didn't see it then. I thought I was just "wired differently." I didn't realise I was self-medicating. That all of it - every pill, every drink, every reckless night - was me trying to drown the symptoms of ADHD I didn't know I had.

Even the stupidest stuff had a reason. Like sneaking out of my bedroom window at night. The adrenaline, the freedom, the dopamine—it was addictive. We'd wander the streets like stray dogs, get into trouble, do whatever kept us stimulated. One night I even snuck people into my downstairs bedroom for a full-blown drug session. The paranoia was intense. Every creak, every shadow, every curtain twitch felt like we were seconds away from getting caught. I must've checked the window every five minutes like I was in a horror film.

But none of it was random. None of it was meaningless. Every risk, every mistake, every bad decision was driven by a need to feel something. A need to escape something. And I didn't even know what that something was.

Only later, much later, did I start putting the pieces together. ADHD. Rejection Sensitive Dysphoria. Emotional dysregulation. It didn't excuse what I did—but it explained it. And that was the beginning of everything finally making sense.

The haze didn't lift right away. But acknowledging it was the first step toward clarity.

A STICKY BEGINNING TO A LIFE LONG FRIENDSHIP.

Picture this: a volcano erupts—not with lava, but with chunky, lukewarm vomit, cascading down the back of my head like something out of Scary Movie. I was five years old, sitting on one of the prized classroom benches, when I got baptised by bile.

The culprit? A pale-looking kid named Ryan.

Turns out the little bugger had been battling some stomach bug and I, lucky me, had unknowingly taken a front-row seat in the splash zone. He projectile vomited with the force of a fire hose. It was less "classroom moment" and more "exorcism scene." You'd think that would've put me off him—or at least off my lunch—but no. That disaster marked the beginning of one of the most ridiculous, chaotic, and loyal friendships of my life.

After the initial shock, and a much-needed shower, it became funny. Like, really funny. What's life without a bit of vomit-induced bonding? That day sealed it. From then on, Ryan and I were inseparable—two peas in a pod, two sides of the same chaotic coin. We spent our lives in tandem, navigating the nonsense of childhood, the mess of adolescence, and the car crash of early adulthood together.

We supported each other through everything—loss, heartbreak, hangovers, and high scores. We always joked to any girls we dated: we come as a package. Two for the price of one. And it was true.

The golden era of our early friendship? The PlayStation 2 years.

We spent night after night glued to my bulky CRT TV—the kind that could crush a small child if it ever toppled off the drawers—losing ourselves in Baldur's Gate: Dark Alliance. The glow of the screen lit up our faces as we navigated dungeons, slayed monsters, and argued over loot. Sleep was optional. Roller cola, Space Raiders, and late-night giggles were mandatory. We'd emerge the next morning bleary-eyed and buzzing, convinced we were elite warriors trapped in teenage bodies.

But our adventures weren't just virtual.

We were absolute little shits if we're being honest. Mischief was our love language. One summer—honestly, it could've been any of them, Ryan basically lived at mine for every six-week holiday—we began a petty crime spree. Our first targets? Dust caps. Yep, car tyre caps. We'd sneak around collecting them like they were Pokémon, laughing like idiots and daring each other to grab more.

Then it escalated. Dust caps got boring. So, we upgraded to car badges.

Armed with a butter knife (for context, the kind you'd spread jam with—not the kind kids today carry for far darker reasons), we prowled the streets in broad daylight or under the cover of night, prising off shiny emblems like we were stealing treasure. The loot lived in my drawer, proudly stashed away like a pirate hoard. Looking back now, yeah—it was dumb. It was illegal. But at the time, it was everything: exciting, stupid, and fuelled by undiagnosed ADHD impulsivity.

Which, funnily enough, we were both diagnosed with in our late twenties.

They say neurodivergent people often find each other. Makes sense now. We'd always understood each other without needing to explain ourselves. The impulsiveness, the restlessness, the inability to just sit still—we shared it all. We weren't bad. We were just trying to manage brains that never stopped buzzing.

That shared chaos carried into our twenties. We'd spend hours driving from pub to pub, "just for one" at each. It was never just one. The Bird in Hand became our HQ. We racked up a tab so consistently, the landlord stopped asking questions. I'd pay it on payday—sometimes it hit £600. It was carnage. Fun, blurry, messy carnage.

When the pubs closed, we weren't ready to stop. If no one else was up for carrying on, Ryan would crash at mine like he always used to. I'd call someone for a bag of coke, and five minutes later, Ryan would be snoring on the sofa—only to sleepwalk and piss on something random. Every time. Caused by too much Sertraline, apparently. Not ideal. But then again, neither was snorting coke every time I'd had a drink. We were both self-medicating in our own chaotic ways, and neither of us knew it.

Somewhere in the madness, we came up with the phrase "lit or quit." It became our life motto. If you weren't living life to the max, what was the point? We pushed limits. Took risks. Genuinely baffled how we didn't kill ourselves—or anyone else.

But consequences always come.

There were the hangovers from hell. The mystery injuries. The memory gaps. We somehow never got pulled for drink driving, which to this day feels like a miracle. Or maybe blind luck. But even through the hangovers, through the regrets, the friendship stood firm.

Then came a shift.

Ryan became a dad. I stopped drinking. The nights got quieter. The tabs disappeared. We started figuring out how to function without wrecking ourselves every weekend. The reckless energy got funnelled into work, family, purpose. But the friendship never faded.

It evolved.

Now, we go weeks without speaking—but when we do, it's like no time has passed. That's how you know it's real. We know each other inside out. We've seen each other at our most unhinged, our most vulnerable, our most "what the hell is wrong with you?" And we've loved each other through it all.

Ryan's not just my mate. He's, my brother. I've known him longer than my own sister's been alive. He's the one constant in a life that's been full of chaos and change.

I think about that a lot—how lucky I am to have had someone ride shotgun through the absolute madness. Someone who never judged me, who laughed when I needed it, who stood by me when I didn't deserve it.

Where would I be without him? No clue.

But I know I wouldn't be me.

And if friendship must start with someone puking on your head—well, I guess I got lucky.

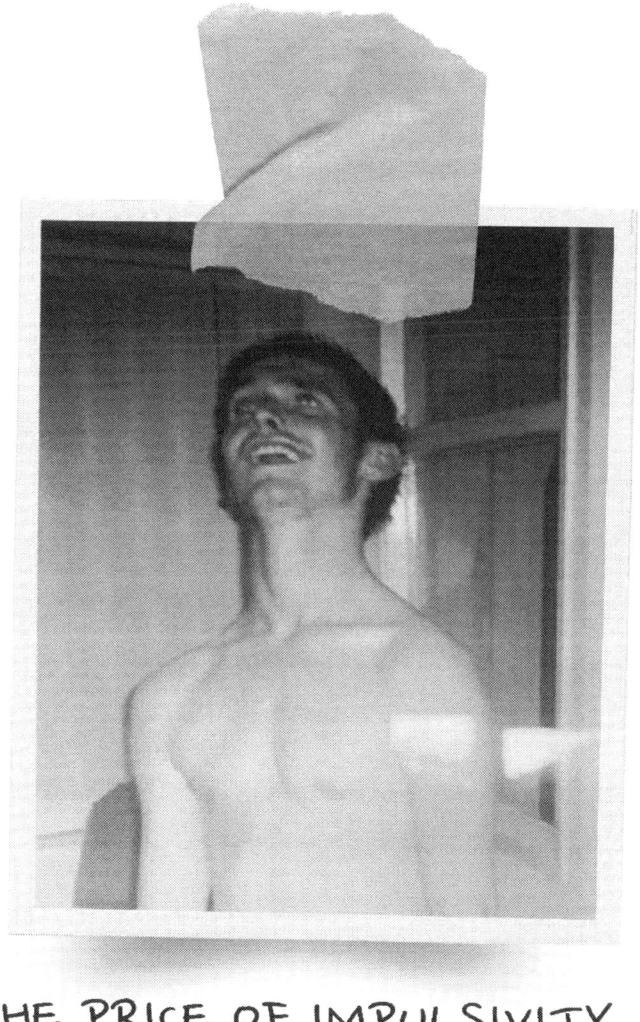

THE PRICE OF IMPULSIVITY.

The first time the cold steel of handcuffs clamped around my wrists, I was still a teenager—a chaotic storm wrapped in skin, hormones, and misfiring impulses. It wasn't a grand crime, not some life-defining act of rebellion. It was just one of those moments, where emotion steamrolled logic.

It started with a stupid argument—two mates, one minor disagreement, and me, completely unable to regulate the flood of emotion that followed. I felt that rage bubbling in my chest, hot and urgent, begging for release. And without thinking, without pausing, I walked over to a parked car and ripped off the rear window wiper like it had personally offended me.

I didn't know then that I was being watched. CCTV operators in Chester had seen the whole performance, likely shaking their heads at yet another teenager blowing up over nothing.

The arrest came quick. Blue lights. Firm voices. Cold cuffs.

The police van ride was quiet. I didn't speak, didn't look at anyone. I felt a cocktail of anger, fear, and embarrassment stirring in my stomach. But nothing compared to the moment the cell door slammed behind me. That sound—that clang—hit harder than any shouting ever could.

Twenty-three hours in a sterile, echoey white cell. A whole day of nothing but the sound of my own thoughts bouncing off concrete walls. No phone. No distractions. Just me, guilt, and silence.

I cried. I'm not ashamed to admit that. Not angry tears—shameful ones. I pictured my mum's face, my dad's disappointment. I knew this wasn't a slap on the wrist anymore. I wasn't the cheeky kid getting dragged home by the collar. This was real. This was serious. And worst of all—I knew they'd tried so hard with me. To guide me. To protect me. And I'd broken that trust. That crushed me more than anything else.

You'd think that would be the turning point.

Looking back, that should have been the wake-up call. A red flag. A clue that my brain didn't work like everyone else's. But back then, no one saw it for what it was. Not even me.

It wasn't the last time I'd actually felt the shame of being treated like a problem.

The second time came not long after.

A bunch of us were out, chasing boredom away like we always did, when someone suggested exploring an abandoned mansion. It had a rep. Rumours said it had once housed a cannabis farm and had been raided a few times. Of course, that made it even more appealing. It was the kind of stupid adventure teenage lads live for.

Creeping through the broken glass, half-whispering and buzzing with adrenaline, we felt invincible. Until the flashing lights cut through the night. Then came the sirens. Then came the helicopter.

We scattered—panicked animals running for cover. I dove into a bush, heart hammering in my chest. The chopper's searchlight cut through the dark like a giant accusing finger. I held my breath, watching shadows dance on the grass. It was like a game of hide and seek, except no one was playing.

They eventually caught me. This time, though, I was smarter—or at least more experienced. I declined a solicitor. I hadn't done anything but wander through a derelict building, and I knew dragging it out would mean hours more in that cell. Still, the fallout was bigger than expected. The police raided my parents' house early the next morning, suspecting us of stealing lead from the mansion's roof. Nothing was found. But it was another black mark. Another instance of my decisions blowing back on people I cared about.

Then there were the club incidents. Fuelled by drink, paranoia, and a deep-rooted sense of insecurity, I started seeing threats that weren't there. Someone looked at the girl I was with? I'd spiral. I'd catastrophise. My brain convinced me it was betrayal, that I wasn't good enough, that I was being laughed at or replaced. That kind of thinking doesn't leave much room for reason.

One night ended with me destroying a hotel room. The aftermath? Police called. Arrested again—this time for breach of the peace. Another cell. Another round of apologies. Another layer of guilt.

But it was the last one that really broke something in me.

It was the night before the second COVID lockdown. The last night the pubs were open. The kind of night people wanted to make count. And I did—just not in the way I should have.

I drank heavily. Planned to get on the coke, numb myself, stay up, keep the chaos going. But I couldn't get hold of any. And that sent me spiralling. I felt out of control, itchy under my own skin. Like I needed something—anything—to quiet the storm.

It hit a nerve so deep I didn't even know it was still there.

Something was said that made me feel inadequate. Useless. Compared. And in that moment, my RSD—Rejection Sensitive Dysphoria—took full control. My brain screamed that I wasn't good enough, never had been, never would be. And then came the rage. Not yelling. Not arguing. But destruction.

I had lost it. The anger I had nowhere to go, and I was slipping. Everyone was scared of the virus – but I was scared of my own mind. I was volatile, unpredictable, and full of noise I couldn't escape. It built up until it exploded.

And when it was over? There was no relief. Just the sound of sirens. The cold steel again. And the same old cell.

That night haunted me for years. It wasn't just about the property damage. It was what it represented. A breaking point. A lifetime of pain and shame and unprocessed trauma finally exploding outward.

I used to drink and use drugs to forget. To escape the guilt of what I'd done and who I thought I was. But you can't outrun guilt. You just carry it further.

These weren't isolated incidents. From my early teens into my twenties, the police became almost routine. From petty nonsense to major consequences—it felt like a cycle I couldn't break.

Until I got diagnosed.

Getting the ADHD diagnosis was like someone finally handed me the instruction manual to my own brain. It didn't fix everything overnight, but it made sense of it. The impulsivity, the rage, the self-sabotage. It wasn't that I didn't care. It was that I couldn't regulate. I wasn't wired to pause. I was wired to react.

As soon as the psychiatrist said it out loud, I froze. My throat closed, my hands started shaking. I wanted to cry, scream, and laugh all at once. For the first time in my life, I had an explanation. It wasn't that I was lazy, broken, or a bad person – my brain just worked differently. I left the room, sat in my car and sobbed. It felt like years of guilt, shame and confusion were trying to leave my body all at once.

Therapy, medication, support—it all helped. Not because it changed who I was, but because it gave me space. Space to think. Space to reflect. Space to choose instead of just explode.

I still carry guilt. I always will. For the things I broke. The people I hurt. The damage I caused—not just to walls or windows, but to relationships, to trust, to my own future.

But I also carry awareness now.

And that's something I never had before.

MKAT AND MADNESS.

The first time I touched MKAT, it felt like I'd unlocked something the rest of the world had kept hidden from me.

It started casually—barely even a decision. Just a line. Just a taste. One cautious line of 4-MMC, snorted in the conservatory of my next-door neighbour's house. The place where I'd once played with action figures now became the lab for a new identity. It was dark outside, I remember that. But the real light came from the inside—the high. The surge of euphoria hit like a lightning bolt to the skull. For the first time in years, I felt alive. Not just okay. Not just existing. Alive.

I didn't just enjoy who I became on it—I preferred that version of myself. Confident, sociable, invincible. My thoughts weren't racing for once, or if they were, it felt like I could keep up. There was no worry, no anxiety, no rejection. Just this beautiful, buzzing clarity. MKAT became my cheat code.

And the best part? It was legal. Over the counter, or straight to your door through the post. A "research chemical," or "plant fertiliser" they called it. All clean and clinical, like it came from a science textbook. No back-alley dealings. No shady street corners. Just powdered freedom with next-day delivery.

Soon enough, it wasn't just a treat. It was the weekend plan. Me and the lads, barely sixteen, drinking in bars like we owned the place—lines in the toilets, nights that bled into mornings. The world became a kaleidoscope. Everything was brighter, funnier, more exciting. Every hug felt like love. Every song was a personal anthem. Every stranger was your best mate.

But the comedowns... that's when it started turning. The glow faded. The paranoia crept in. And worst of all, I wanted more. Desperately. Because once you've felt like a god, coming back down to earth is unbearable.

That's when my life began to shift from one of promise to one of pursuit.

The apprenticeship that had once felt like the start of something real now came second to the hunt. I'd fake sick days with a sore throat voice and an apologetic tone, phone in excuses while scraping powder out of a bag in my room. I was becoming someone else—someone I didn't fully recognise but couldn't stop being.

The Scout Hut became our headquarters. I'd gone from earning badges there as a kid to turning it into a haven of drug-fuelled escape. The same walls that once echoed with laughter and lessons now reverberated with basslines, muffled laughter, and the snort of crushed crystals. Cigarette smoke hung thick, the air heavy with chemicals and chaos. It wasn't just getting high—it was getting lost.

I drifted from the boy I was. My relationship with my high school sweetheart—something pure and grounding—fell apart. She couldn't understand why I was becoming so erratic, so shut off. I couldn't either. One minute I was euphoric, the next I was numb. Mood swings, isolation, bursts of anger. I pushed her away until there was nothing left.

What followed wasn't romance—it was transactions. Girls came and went. Not because of me, but because of what I could offer. Drugs. Escapism. I was just a means to a high, and somewhere in that mess, I stopped expecting more. My bedroom became a revolving door of fleeting encounters. I felt like a stray cat—unwelcome in the daylight, only coming to life when the sun went down.

My next-door neighbour—my childhood partner in crime—became my right hand in destruction. Our nights followed a pattern: pub, line, plan. If his mum was home, we'd take it back to mine. If mine was home, we'd head to the Scout Hut. It didn't matter. We just needed somewhere to chase the high. The location changed, but the mission never did.

I started dealing, too.

One time, I bought an ounce off a dealer with a promise to pay later. Of course, I dipped into it. Told myself I'd pay it back. But before I knew it, I'd sniffed most of it, and I still owed. This wasn't the type of guy you make excuses to. He wasn't known for his patience—and he certainly wasn't known for forgiveness.

I panicked.

Desperate to make it right, I broke into the house of a mate who owed me money, hoping to recover something I could use to pay the dealer back. I wasn't even scared anymore—I was just functioning on survival mode. The guilt came later. The shame came later. In the moment, all that mattered was the next gram and staying alive.

Strangely, instead of punishing me, the dealer admired the boldness. He took me under his wing. Suddenly, I wasn't just a user. I was in the business.

We became a unit—cruising around, selling to anyone and everyone. The Scout Hut wasn't just a hideout anymore—it was the HQ. We threw parties that lasted all night. The smell of stale beer, smoke, sweat, and chemicals clung to the walls. Bags on the table. Notes and cards passed around. Everyone chasing something.

The physical signs of addiction crept in slowly. My face got thinner. My clothes hung looser. I couldn't breathe properly. Constant sniffing. Nosebleeds. Massive scabs from where the powder had burned inside my nostrils. I looked like someone falling apart—and I was.

I would sit in my room for hours, curtains drawn, just racking up lines. Days passed without me knowing what day it was. Sleep was optional. Food was forgotten. My body was breaking down, but my brain was still screaming for more.

To fund it, I borrowed. Lied. Took payday loans. Sold anything not nailed down. I'd call mates or family with fake emergencies, promising to pay it back. I rarely did. The guilt would hit me later, but in the moment, it was just one more fix, one more line, one more temporary relief.

The paranoia kicked in hard. I'd think shadows were people. Think the police were watching. Think my phone was tapped. I couldn't sit still. I couldn't relax. I was stuck in a state of constant hyper-awareness. It was exhausting. It was terrifying. And I still couldn't stop.

MKAT, the drug that once made me feel limitless, had trapped me. I was no longer in control—I was a passenger in my own life, watching the wreckage build up around me.

Then it started getting harder to get hold of. Laws changed. Supplies dried up. And right on cue, something worse slid onto the scene.

Cocaine.

If MKAT was the devil I knew, cocaine was the devil with an even bigger smile. It hit harder, felt cleaner, and burned through my brain faster. I embraced it like an old friend, eager to lose myself all over again.

Because at that point, I didn't care about recovery. I didn't care about the future. I just wanted the noise in my head to stop. I just wanted to feel like someone again.

What began as an experiment had turned into survival.

And I was losing.

THE PRICE OF PASSION.

The late teen years are intense for anyone, but for me—with undiagnosed ADHD fuelling every high and crashing every low—they were absolute chaos. My love life reflected that chaos: fast, fiery, impulsive, and completely unsustainable.

Every relationship I had during that time was a high-speed emotional rollercoaster—no seatbelt, no brakes, and usually no clear reason for why it began or ended. One week I'd be falling head over heels, obsessively attentive, convinced I'd found the one. The next, I'd already be moving on, chasing a new feeling, a new rush, a new someone. It wasn't just attraction—it was infatuation, always intense, always immediate, and usually short-lived. I was trying to fill a void I didn't understand.

I thought love was something you proved through grand gestures. I didn't know how to just be with someone. I thought spending money, buying gifts, and overcompensating with attention would make me enough. But the more I gave, the more drained I became. And when things didn't work out, which they rarely did, I didn't just feel sad—I felt like I'd failed on a fundamental level. That something was broken in me.

One girl I'll never forget—brown hair, sharp wit, eyes that didn't take bullshit. She was known around Chester, a bit of a local personality. When we got together, I was stunned. I didn't understand what she saw in me. But that didn't stop me from diving in headfirst. I poured everything into her.

Time, energy, money, attention. If she wanted it, I got it. If she was sad, I fixed it. If she was angry, I took it.

But she carried her own demons. She was jealous—deeply, irrationally so. If I listened to a song with a female singer, she'd spiral, convinced I fancied the artist. She'd rage over music choices, over glances, over people I'd never even spoken to. I'd try to reason with her, but logic had no place in jealousy. Still, I tried. I adjusted everything to make her feel secure, to avoid conflict, to keep the peace.

Looking back, I wasn't keeping the peace—I was just losing myself. Years later, we met again. Older. Wiser. Calmer. We sat down, talked things out, and made peace. Age gives you perspective that teenage chaos never could. We even laughed. And then I got blackout drunk, and she ended up driving me home—despite me being the one supposed to be sober for work the next day. I'd planned to drive myself. She saved me, again. That's how life works sometimes messy but poetic.

Another girl, different story. Our fights were volcanic. One night, after an argument, I slammed the car door shut so hard the window shattered. A shard of glass flew into her arm, cutting her deep. I was horrified. Absolutely crushed by what I'd done. I apologised instantly, panicked, shaking. But apologies don't rewind time. She was left with a scar—on her skin and in her memory. So was I.

That same relationship took a darker turn one night when I hit my lowest emotional point. Drunk, heart racing, completely overwhelmed, I stormed off and ended up back at hers. I was spiralling. Couldn't regulate my emotions. Couldn't stop the storm inside. In a moment of madness, I took a penknife to my own arm. I missed a vein by millimetres. It turned yellow, spread with infection, and I told no one. My parents were away. When they got back, I denied everything.

The scariest part? It wasn't a cry for help. It was a desperate attempt to feel something. To stop the pain in my head by making pain somewhere else. I didn't want to die—I just didn't want to feel like that anymore.

Drugs made it all worse. Cocaine, especially. It didn't just fuel the anger and impulsivity—it numbed the aftermath. That was part of the addiction: not just the high, but the ability to switch off. To stop feeling. I'd say the worst things to people. Start arguments with strangers. Accuse anyone I perceived as a threat. Sometimes it was protectiveness. Mostly, it was paranoia.

In my head, if people thought I was dangerous, they'd leave me alone. I didn't realise I was pushing people away who were never trying to hurt me in the first place. And the people I did scare off? I wore that like armour. If I could be feared, I wouldn't be rejected.

From 17 to 20, I burned through five or six relationships. All intense. All short. Most with brunettes—no real pattern beyond that. Each girl completely different, but I treated every relationship the same. Obsessive attention, desperate need for approval, big emotional swings, and then a total cut-off when things went wrong.

I had this ability to switch off. I could erase people like they never existed. One minute I'd be heartbroken. The next, I'd be fine. Not because I was cold—but because I couldn't handle the sadness. Numbness felt easier. Cocaine helped with that. It helped with everything. Until it helped with nothing.

I didn't know how to be alone. I couldn't stand it. Silence was unbearable. Boredom was torture. I needed constant validation to feel like I mattered. Being in a relationship meant I was wanted. Needed. Seen. And if I was pleasing someone else, I didn't have to think about how empty I felt inside.

The problem was, I didn't know who I was. So, I lost myself in whoever I was dating. I moulded myself to fit their needs. Their moods. Their expectations. I made them my entire world—until it fell apart. Then I'd move on. Try again. Same script. Different cast.

It's easy to blame ADHD. And yeah, it played a big role—impulsivity, rejection sensitivity, emotional dysregulation. All of it was in the mix. But there was more to it, too. I was broken in ways I didn't understand. Trying to patch myself up with relationships that weren't equipped to carry that weight.

I didn't need a girlfriend.

I needed to heal.

SPIRALING OUT OF LOVE.

It started like so many of my relationships did: suddenly, passionately, and with zero regard for the fallout. She came into my life through a mutual work friend—free-spirited, chaotic, wild-eyed, and magnetic. She described herself as "untameable," and to someone like me—wired for intensity, obsessed with the idea of saving people—it felt less like a red flag and more like a challenge.

We moved fast. Too fast. Within weeks I'd ditched my space, my routine, and moved into her student accommodation. We didn't so much fall into a relationship as collide into one. Everything was adrenaline. Passion. Late-night walks through the streets of Liverpool, off our faces at 4am, hands locked together like some tragic Bonnie and Clyde. Hotel rooms packed with people and substances I hadn't even heard of—GHB, "geebs," and all sorts of alphabet soup that came in little baggies. We told ourselves it wasn't going to be a party lifestyle. But that's exactly what it became: one long, sleepless, chaotic party we couldn't stop attending.

When she dropped out of university—no qualifications, no plan—I was all in. I told her not to worry, that I made enough to support us both. That I'd look after her. That she didn't need a plan because I was the plan. Truth is, I was more focused on being the rescuer than I was on seeing the truth. I didn't know her. Not really. I knew her in the sesh, in the chaos, in the afterglow of wild nights. But I didn't know her when the drugs wore off. Neither of us knew each other sober.

Reality came crashing in one night at Pop world. She'd gotten into it with someone and, ever the protector, I stepped in. A bouncer didn't like it and decided to make an example of me—chucking me down the stairs like a sack of rubbish. I cracked my head so hard it took staples to close it. A&E told me, the alcohol in my system might have been the only reason I wasn't paralysed. Apparently, being that drunk made me limp enough not to snap my neck. Funny how close you can come to disaster and still walk away. Just.

We thought a change of scenery might help, so we moved into a house on a new-build estate in Norris Green. She liked it—close to her mates—and I, as usual, put her happiness before mine. Even though I felt completely out of place, even though I isolated myself to make it work, I stayed. That's what I did—I endured to earn love.

Then my Subaru got stolen.

I was at a retirement do, half-cut and feeling good for once, when my phone rang. The police. Calling from my house phone. They thought we'd been taken hostage. They'd put the front door through and everything. She was at my parents.' I was in town. No one had been home. The car was just gone, and the police had wrecked the house trying to "save" us.

I panicked. Jumped in a cab with a workmate and legged it back to Norris Green. When we arrived, a slow-moving car crept past the house. Without thinking—high, drunk, and angry—I sprinted after it. I didn't catch it, of course. But what if I had? What if there'd been a weapon? A gun? I didn't care. I didn't think. That's what my impulsivity does—it puts me in danger and makes me think I'm invincible.

The arguments at home turned violent. I smashed a pint glass underneath my right hand, and when the glass smashed underneath, it had nowhere to shatter, and a piece of glass sliced straight through the muscle in my thumb. Blood everywhere.

Another night, the police showed up after the neighbours reported the noise. One wall was completely caved in. The house was becoming a war zone—cocaine-fuelled midweek rows, weekend parties, and a growing list of lies between us. Infidelity crept in, both ways, both hidden but sensed. We knew. We just didn't say it out loud. Like if we ignored it, it couldn't hurt us.

Then came the messages.

I'd just got into bed after a long day. I was knackered and had to be up for work at 6am. I'd done her a favour—picked her and a mate up from a rave in Manchester, dropped them home, and come back to crash. But something wouldn't let me sleep. A gut feeling. So, I opened her social media, scrolled through the DMs—and there it was. Multiple messages to men, telling them to come over for a "good time" as soon as I left for work.

I couldn't breathe.

When I confronted her, she barely looked guilty. She just panicked about her Louis Vuitton bag. "But you promised to buy it with your bonus," she said, completely unfazed by the betrayal. It was like I wasn't even real to her. I was just a payday, a body, a lift home.

I snapped. Told her we were done. Got her and her mate back in the car and drove them to the friend's house. The silence was thick, the tension worse than anything we'd said. Then, in the middle of the drive, she tried to throw herself out of the moving car.

We were going 60mph.

I slammed the brakes, heart pounding, adrenaline roaring in my ears. She was kicking, screaming, trying to escape. I physically pulled her back in, slammed the door shut, and begged her to stop. It was chaos. Madness. The lowest point of an already tragic love story.

And yet... a few days later, I took her back.

Why? Because I blamed myself. Because I was used to broken love. Because I still hoped something good could come from the wreckage. But it was a mistake, and one I'd come to regret deeply.

The darkest moment came later—an unwanted pregnancy, ended in silence and shame. I still don't know if it was mine. She'd cheated on me with her boss, a truth I only discovered after the fact. But it didn't matter. I remember the day vividly. The clinical, brutal reality. The image of that tiny, alien-like foetus. The sound of it being flushed. I still hear it sometimes when I try to sleep. That moment sits in me like a weight I'll carry forever.

We tried to pretend things were okay. I even gave counselling a go—until I realised one of the men, she'd slept with was sitting across the table from me in group therapy. That was the end of that. I walked out and never went back.

Our final move was desperate. We relocated to a quiet village—the same one I'd gone to primary school in—thinking a fresh start might help. But it didn't. If anything, it amplified everything. I was now living steps away from the pub I used to drink in. She felt isolated. I became a regular again. Part of the furniture. Numbing myself nightly, chasing oblivion with a pint and a line.

Eventually, it ended. Properly this time. No more fake restarts, no more empty promises. Just silence.

After she left, my best mate moved in to help me cope. But I was lost. A shell of myself. Alone, grieving, drinking, sniffing. That house—our "fresh start"—became a shrine to everything I'd destroyed.

And the worst part?

I still believed I deserved it.

THE ILLUSION OF GRANDEUR.

Before my diagnosis, life felt like a blur viewed through frosted glass—hazy, disjointed, and dangerously disconnected. I didn't know it at the time, but undiagnosed ADHD was steering the wheel while I was in the back seat, busy performing for a crowd I'd imagined in my head. Every decision, every night out, every absurd purchase, was part of a performance—a show to prove that I was someone. Someone worthy. Someone important.

The reality? I was chasing smoke.

What I craved more than anything was validation. Approval. To feel like I mattered. And in the absence of knowing how to earn it honestly, I turned to illusion. Flashy clothes. Loud entrances. Champagne, I didn't even like. Anything that made me look like I had my life together, even as it unravelled in the background.

I still remember the night I hit one of those peaks of pretence.

I was at a local nightclub, standing in the so-called VIP area. It was hardly the Ritz—just a sectioned-off part of a mirrored bar with velvet ropes and dim neon lighting that reflected everything except reality. In a moment of ego-fuelled madness, I ordered a 70cl bottle of Belvedere vodka. Price tag? Over a hundred quid. You can buy it for twenty in Tesco. But that wasn't the point. It wasn't about the drink—

it was about the image. The bottle gleamed under the lights, and for a second, so did I.

Then I got into a scuffle with a stranger. Something minor. Some meaningless look or bump or misread gesture. But when your self-worth is hanging by a thread, everything feels like a threat. It escalated quickly—words, then fists—and I don't even remember the exact moment I went down. One second, I was in the booth, the next I was being carried out, limp, bloodied, and dumped down the street like a bin bag on collection day. The Belvedere, I imagine, lay smashed in a puddle of vodka and shattered pride. I was drunk, humiliated, and half-conscious. And still, the next time I went out, I tried again. Because that's what you do when you're chasing something that doesn't exist.

Designer labels became another obsession. Christian Louboutin's, £1,000 price tags, underwear so tight it felt like punishment. I didn't even like most of it. But it made me feel expensive. I thought it'd raise my value in the eyes of others. Watches, jeans, coats—I built an entire identity out of cotton and leather, hoping someone would notice. Hoping I would believe the hype.

Most of the time, I didn't even drink what I bought. VIP tables littered with untouched bottles of Grey Goose and Patron, because it wasn't about consuming—it was about being seen. I wanted people to think I was successful. Put-together. Someone to envy. But behind all that? I couldn't even pay my phone bill.

One night, a woman—just a friend of a friend—looked at me differently. Not with awe or admiration, but with understanding. She didn't see Maddog the "baller." She saw the lad trying far too hard to be someone he wasn't. She said it gently—almost kindly—but it hit like a punch in the gut. I laughed it off, turned up the volume, tried to outshine the truth. But deep down, I knew she was right. The version of me I was selling wasn't real. He was stitched together with desperation and debt.

At my worst, I genuinely thought carrying around a magnum of Grey Goose made me look sophisticated. That I was some sort of mysterious, high-rolling legend. One night, I tried sneaking one out of a club by stuffing it down my trouser leg like I was smuggling contraband out of Colditz. Predictably, I got caught. In a flash of rage and idiocy, I hurled it at the bouncers. Glass exploded across the floor, vodka soaking the walls. The bottle I'd prized so highly—now just a symbol of how pathetic it had all become.

And still, I kept going.

I'd buy bottles for strangers on their birthdays, trying to win affection with money I didn't have. I thought it'd make people like me. It didn't. I thought it'd build connections. It didn't. All it did was empty my pockets and leave me surrounded by people who disappeared the moment I stopped paying. Everyone was my best mate until the bank balance hit zero. Then I became invisible.

The most ridiculous part? I didn't even like champagne. But that didn't stop me parading around clubs with a bottle of Dom Pérignon tucked under my arm like I was James Bond. It wasn't about taste. It was about status. I convinced myself it made me look sophisticated, important. In reality, I just looked like a twat. A walking contradiction—dripping in labels, drowning in insecurity.

I was the textbook definition of a "Grey Goose wanker."

Working shifts gave me weird stretches of freedom—six days off at a time. That freedom became fuel. Midweek benders, random Tuesday night madness, thousands of pounds burned through like it was Monopoly money. The morning after always came like a cold slap. I'd wake up in bed, heart racing, bank balance in ruins, wondering how the hell it happened again.

I knew, of course.

It was the ADHD. The impulsivity. The need for stimulation. The hatred of silence and stillness. But back then, I didn't have a name for it. All I knew was that if I wasn't doing something big, I didn't feel real. And the only thing that kept me going through nights like that was cocaine. Without it, I'd have been passed out in a gutter. With it, I could keep performing. Keep pretending. Keep the illusion alive.

And it was never about attracting girls. It actually did the opposite—most women saw through the act. The ones who didn't were often chasing illusions of their own. This wasn't for them. It wasn't even for my mates. They didn't care whether I wore Louboutin's or Asda socks. This was for me. It was me trying to impress myself. Trying to believe that I was someone worth looking at.

But the more I tried to inflate my image, the smaller I felt. It chipped away at me. Slowly, relentlessly. Until I didn't know who I was underneath it all.

The illusion of grandeur was just that—an illusion. Smoke and mirrors. I wore it like a mask because I hated what was underneath. I needed people to believe I was something, because I couldn't bear the thought of being nothing.

And the craziest part? It worked. For a while. People bought the act. Some envied it. Some wanted to be part of it. But none of them knew me. Not really.

How could they? I didn't even know myself.

Only after my diagnosis did things start to make sense. The impulsivity. The need to impress. The shame-fuelled spending. It wasn't just poor choices. It was brain chemistry. Years of untreated ADHD, masked with a smile and a platinum Amex.

Now I look back and laugh—but also, I grieve. For the time wasted. For the person I was trying so hard to become. For the young man screaming for approval and never knowing how to ask for help.

Maddog wasn't who I was.

He was who I thought I had to be.

And that illusion nearly broke me.

THE SOCIAL MEDIA TRAP.

Social media: the great connector. Or so they say.

A world built on the promise of community, validation, and staying "in the loop." But what it became for me was something far more sinister—a daily reminder that I wasn't enough.

What starts as a scroll becomes a spiral. You hop on for a quick look and suddenly you're lost in someone else's highlight reel. Exotic holidays. Gym selfies. Happy families. Engagement announcements. New houses. Six-figure businesses. And there I was, slouched on the couch, checking my overdraft limit, eating cereal out of a mixing bowl at 2 p.m.

They say comparison is the thief of joy—but social media is the getaway driver.

Every post felt like a jab. Every like on someone else's life chipped away at mine. And it didn't even matter if I knew the person. I'd compare myself to a guy I'd never met, living in Dubai with a jawline carved from granite, driving a rented Lambo and quoting fake motivational captions like, "Hustle in silence." And there I was, hustling in debt. Loudly.

I didn't realise it at the time, but I was measuring my behind-the-scenes against everyone else's front-of-house. Their curated lives vs. my chaos. And I always came up short.

Even messaging platforms weren't safe. WhatsApp became a new layer of anxiety. Being left on read? Pure emotional sabotage. Double texting? Triple texting? A full-blown internal war. "Did I say too much?" "Did I sound needy?" "Why haven't they replied?" I'd re-read messages like a crime scene detective looking for the one thing I said wrong. A simple delay in reply could trigger a full-blown spiral—rejection, self-loathing, overthinking. All of it wrapped up in the fear that I was being ignored on purpose.

I knew deep down this wasn't normal, but knowing didn't stop the feeling. ADHD and anxiety together make a mess of logic. I wasn't waiting for a text—I was holding my breath for validation.

The pressure to keep up online became exhausting. Not just to post. To perform. You don't just exist online—you present. You frame, filter, tweak. Even the most candid photos are rehearsed. And for what? Likes from people I barely knew. Virtual applause that faded as fast as it came?

I was trying to impress people who probably wouldn't recognise me in Tesco without a filter.

Eventually, I hit a wall.

I deleted everything—Facebook, Instagram, Snapchat. Turned off read receipts. Disabled "last seen." Nuked the entire operation. Just shut it all down. WhatsApp became purely functional. No more checking if someone had opened a message. If they had, fine. If not, fine. I had to stop obsessing over things that weren't real threats.

And honestly, it felt like a detox. Not the trendy kind with smoothies and overpriced candles. A real one. From bullshit. From comparison. From noise. I felt calmer. Quieter. More grounded. The tension in my chest eased. I wasn't constantly chasing someone else's life—I was starting to live my own again.

Of course, it came with its own set of problems. Try telling a girl on Tinder you don't have Instagram. "Oh, you're either married or you're a catfish." Brilliant. I had to send photos of myself doing weird things just to prove I wasn't AI-generated. Holding up a spoon to my forehead. Balancing a shoe on my head. Like some twisted audition for Britain's Most Normal Bloke. Cheers, Zuckerberg.

But the biggest shift came when I launched Attentive.

Suddenly, I had to rejoin the very world I'd run from. Social media wasn't a distraction anymore—it was my business. My story. My voice. And as it turns out, people wanted to hear it. The comments started pouring in. Videos went viral. DMs from people saying I'd helped them feel seen. That my honesty helped them understand their ADHD. It was incredible.

Until it wasn't.

Because along with the love came the trolls.

The ones who hide behind anonymous profiles. Who say things they'd never dare say to your face. The ones who mock neurodivergence like it's a punchline. Who ridicule what they don't understand. Who throw poison into a comment box because it's easier than facing their own pain.

One bloke from Texas said something vile. I was so triggered I nearly booked a flight. I caught myself mid-rage, halfway through typing a message back. That's the ADHD trap—someone lights the fuse, and our fight-or-flight kicks in before we can think.

You go from calm to feral in 0.3 seconds. Logic? Gone. Perspective? Out the window. All that matters is responding, defending, attacking. It's not about ego—it's about survival. Your brain thinks it's being threatened.

And that's where social media can be lethal for people like me.

We don't just see a comment—we feel it. We live inside it. Obsess over it. Rehearse responses. Internalise insults. Give complete strangers space in our heads for days.

But the truth is, the ones who type the worst things are usually the ones hurting the most. The ones with no profile picture. The ones with names like @xx_GhostSlayer420_xx. They're not well. They're not whole. And their opinion? It's not worth your peace.

What I've learned is this: social media is a tool. It can build or break. Connect or isolate. It's all about how you use it. Set boundaries. Take breaks. Don't engage with trolls. Turn off what doesn't serve you.

And remember—the life that really matters isn't behind a screen. It's in the conversations you have face to face. It's in the moments that don't need to be posted. It's in your growth, your stillness, your presence.

The world online might be filtered and polished—but the real you? The one in joggers at 3pm making a brew, fighting your demons, showing up anyway?

That's the version that deserves love.

That's the version that's real.

THE FOG OF
MISUNDERSTANDING.

My childhood home was filled with love—but that love often got lost in translation.

There was no shortage of support, no absence of meals or warmth or clothes on my back. But there was a fog that lingered over everything. A fog made of misunderstanding, confusion, and silence. Not because my parents didn't care. They cared deeply. But because we were all trying to navigate something none of us could see.

My undiagnosed ADHD wasn't loud and obvious. I wasn't "the naughty boy" at school. I wasn't getting detentions, or flipping tables, or screaming for attention in class. I was masking—quiet, sometimes withdrawn, trying hard to fit in, to fly under the radar. So, the chaos that lived inside me? It stayed hidden. Until it couldn't anymore.

At home, it would erupt. Like a bottle that had been shaken all day and finally cracked open. It could be a single comment, a sudden change in tone, a look I misread on someone's face—and I'd explode. The emotional surges were tidal. One minute I was laughing, the next I was screaming, slamming doors, lashing out. I didn't understand why. Neither did they.

I often wonder what it must've been like for my parents. Watching their happy, energetic son turn on a dime. Seeing joy turn to rage with no warning, no roadmap. I imagine the fear in their eyes. The helplessness. The guilt. The anger. How could they help when they didn't even know what they were dealing with?

My mum was my safe place—and the one who bore the brunt of my storms. She's always been the closest person to me. Our bond has weathered everything. But in those moments, she was often the target. I didn't mean to hurt her. But in the chaos of an emotional outburst, she was the closest thing, the softest target. And when you're a child feeling so out of control, you aim for whatever might bring it back.

She tried. She really tried. But back then, understanding children's mental health or neurodivergence wasn't what it is now. ADHD was a buzzword for "naughty boys who couldn't sit still." Not quiet boys who felt everything at 300%. So, when I acted out—when I pushed boundaries or exploded over something small—her discipline came from a place of desperation. A smack on the bum. A warning I wouldn't sit down for a week. It was never out of cruelty. It was frustration. Helplessness. That heartbreaking point parents reach when nothing seems to work.

And I was hard work. I know that now. But I also know it wasn't because I was a "bad kid." I was overwhelmed. Understood by no one, including myself. Sometimes I'd push so far, so hard, that things crossed a line—like the time I pulled a knife on my mum. I didn't intend to use it. But the fact that it happened at all? That I even thought to do something like that? It's something I still carry. I regret it deeply. I was a child—but the damage was very real.

My dad? He was a different type of parent. The provider. The man who went to work, put food on the table, and expected things to run smoothly. He came from a generation where men didn't show emotion. Where crying was weakness. Where feelings were handled with silence or a pint at the pub. And yet, even though he would say, "It's okay to cry," I rarely saw him do it. And as a kid who worked off actions, not words, that message never quite landed.

I wanted time with him. I needed it. But he didn't know how to give it in the way I needed. He wanted structure, logic, clear thinking. I was emotional, chaotic, reactive. I think he saw me as unpredictable—and I saw him as distant. That gap between us only grew over time, especially as my meltdowns got worse. I'd act out, he'd try to discipline, I'd push back harder. The cycle repeated.

Sometimes I'd play them off each other, twisting the narrative to get my way. I'd tell one thing to my mum, the opposite to my dad. Stirring the pot, trying to tip the scales in my favour. Not out of malice—but because I was desperate to feel some sort of control. Some say in a world that felt stacked against me.

And yet, despite all of this, they never stopped loving me.

They taught me to work hard, to be loyal, to take responsibility—even when I failed at it. They never gave up. Not when I dropped out of school. Not when I raged at them. Not even when I got physical and crossed a line I can't undo.

That fog of misunderstanding became heaviest in my teenage years. The ADHD was intensifying, and the stakes were higher. I became hypersensitive to rejection, to broken promises—especially from the people I needed most. One time, I was promised sweets after school. But when the day ended and I didn't get them, I was devastated. It sounds ridiculous, right? But for a kid like me, it felt like betrayal. A small crack that echoed into adulthood. It taught me not to trust. Not fully. Not even the people who loved me most.

And then came the nuclear moment.

There was a time when my family changed in a way I didn't see coming. As a kid, I didn't fully understand what was going on – only that things between my parents suddenly weren't the same. The house felt colder. My dad seemed distant. My mum was hurting in her own way too. Looking back now as an adult, I can see how complicated love and relationships really are. But at the time, it felt like the ground underneath me had cracked.

Finding out was like being struck by lightning. She was my rock. My constant. The one person I never thought would hurt me. And suddenly, that belief shattered. I was blinded by rage, betrayal, heartbreak. I remember grabbing a baseball bat and chasing her down the street. Not because I wanted to hurt her, but because I needed her to feel what I felt. And the worst part? I was the one who told my dad, about what she had done.

I'd never seen him cry before. But that day, he crumbled. And I hated it. I hated watching the strongest man I knew break in front of me. Hated being the reason it happened. Even though she'd made the mistake, I delivered the blow. That moment burned a hole in all of us.

My relationship with my dad would fracture further after that. One night, during a blazing row, I lashed out and hit him. I don't remember what triggered it. All I remember is the look in his eyes. Hurt. Disappointment. And then the cold silence that followed. I was kicked out. Multiple times. And every time, it felt like I was proving the worst things he feared about me.

But here's what's important—we came back.

And then there were the times he found out I was using drugs. Each time, it felt less like a concern and more like a condemnation. He gave me an ultimatum – stop or be disowned. As if I was doing it for fun. As if I enjoyed being an addict. That cut deeper than most things ever have. Because what I needed wasn't more shame or threats – I needed support. I needed someone to see past the behaviour and ask why I felt the need to do them and be numbing myself in the first place. I wasn't trying to ruin anyone's life. I was trying to survive mine. But in this world, it didn't fit the narrative. I didn't fit the narrative. Instead of being helped, I was nearly erased.

Somehow, through all the chaos, the shouting, the heartbreak, my parents never gave up on me. And I never stopped loving them. It just took me longer to understand how to love them properly. It took getting diagnosed. It took understanding why I was the way I was.

Now? Our relationship is stronger than it's ever been.

We talk openly. We reflect. We laugh about the madness. We cry when we need to. I get it now. Why they reacted the way they did. Why they struggled. They weren't perfect—but they were present. They didn't always understand me—but they tried. And sometimes, that's more than enough.

Becoming a father, myself has made that even clearer. Now I hear their voices in mine. Now I say the same things I used to roll my eyes at. And I realise—it wasn't control. It was care. They just didn't know how to say it in a language I understood at the time.

They were right about most things.

I just wasn't ready to listen.

THE GRIND NEVER STOPPED.

My mind has never known quiet. Even as a kid, there was always something buzzing—thoughts racing, ideas crashing into each other like dodgems at full speed. I didn't know why I felt so different. So, on edge. So unable to just be. The grind didn't start when I became an adult—it started way before that. And not because I had some big plan, but because I didn't know how else to exist.

At twelve, while other kids were still figuring out how to tie their ties properly for school, I was out in the freezing cold at the crack of dawn, launching newspapers into letterboxes like frisbees. Rain, shine, sleet—it didn't matter. I had a job to do. I didn't think of it as "character building" at the time. I just knew that work meant money, and money meant freedom. And freedom? That was the one thing I craved more than anything.

By thirteen, I'd upgraded from newspapers to pub work—starting off as a pot washer and a glass collector in a local pub that would end up playing a massive role in my life. That place became my second home. A weird one, sure, but a home, nonetheless. I'd scrub pans until my fingers shrivelled and then go clear pints off sticky tables from half-drunk regulars who thought they were philosophers.

As I got older, the marigolds came off, and the pint glasses went up. I became a waiter. With that came tips, late-night laughs, and Strongbow ciders handed to me like gold medals at the end of a shift. I was underage, yeah—but in that place, nobody really cared. If you grafted, you were accepted. That pub was the first place where I felt like I wasn't "too much." I had a role. A routine. A reason to be.

I joined the darts team not long after. I wasn't exactly Phil Taylor, but it gave me something to pour my obsession into. I had this need to be good at something—anything. That quiet fire in my chest to prove myself, to show I was more than just the hyperactive kid with a short fuse. That pub was the training ground for all of it—how to work hard, how to read people, how to blend in when your brain is screaming at you from the inside.

But don't get me wrong—I wasn't some angelic model employee. Far from it.

I had my own little games. Like the "extra tally" trick. Every dessert I sold, I'd sometimes sneak an extra chalk mark on the board. Each one meant an extra 20p at the end of the week. It wasn't much, but for a teenager with undiagnosed ADHD and a mild obsession with sweets and scheming, it felt like I was cracking the code. Just another dopamine hit disguised as a work ethic.

Then there were the late-night fridge raids.

When the place was locked up and the staff had gone, I'd grab a couple of mates, and we'd hop the side wall like burglars in a low-budget film. The adrenaline of dodging the cameras, sneaking into the stock room, and emerging with beer and ice cream—it was like our own little heist. We weren't smashing windows or robbing tills. But still, we knew what we were doing. And we loved it.

It wasn't about theft. It was about freedom. Stimulation. Rebellion against the repetitive, grey day-to-day life we felt stuck in. For a kid like me—wired differently, constantly seeking something to feel—routine felt like suffocation. So, I made my own fun, even if it was a bit dodgy.

At school, I was still masking. Still smiling. Still being polite and cracking jokes, blending in with the teachers and the kids. But inside? I was drowning in noise. Focus was a nightmare. Motivation came in bursts—like fireworks. Bright, powerful, but gone in seconds. I could charm the room but couldn't finish a homework sheet. I could stay up all night stacking chairs and cleaning kitchens but couldn't sit through a 40-minute lesson.

I became the king of people-pleasing. I knew how to wear the mask. Knew how to be who people needed me to be. Teachers liked me. Managers liked me. Customers tipped me. Nobody saw the chaos behind the charm. I was like a swan—graceful on the surface, legs kicking like mad underneath just to stay afloat.

My jobs piled up as I got older—waiting tables, cooking, front of house. I always said yes to more shifts, more roles, more responsibility. Not because I was ambitious, but because I didn't know how to stop. Stillness felt like death. If I had a free evening, I didn't rest—I filled it. If I didn't, my brain would. And trust me, you don't want to be alone with a brain like mine when it's idle.

But as much as I worked, the mistakes came with me. I'd say the wrong thing, forget the right thing, act on impulse, and regret it immediately. I'd promise to be on time and show up an hour late. I'd get told off for something minor and spiral like the world was ending. I lived in constant fear of being found out—that people would realise I wasn't as capable as I pretended to be.

I was grafting like a man with five kids and a mortgage. I was still a teenager.

Looking back now, I see the signs clear as day. The hyperactivity. The obsessive work ethic. The dopamine chases. The bending of rules. The impulsive risks. It wasn't just "being a character." It was ADHD, screaming for attention before I even knew its name.

But if there's one thing, I'm grateful for, it's that even in all that chaos—I never stopped moving forward. Never stopped working. Never gave up on myself completely.

Because when everything else fell apart—school, relationships, my mental health—I still had the grind. The shift. The reason to get up and do something.

And some days, that was enough.

SWIPING THROUGH THE VOID.

Freedom from a toxic relationship is supposed to feel like a clean break—like opening a window after years of breathing in second-hand smoke. But when you've spent your life surviving chaos, peace feels unnerving. Quiet becomes suspicious. So, when I got out of that chapter of my life, I didn't feel relief. I felt lost.

So, I did what I always did—I filled the space. I called up Ryan, my longest-serving partner in crime, and asked him to move in with me. We'd been through enough together to write our own sitcom—except this one came with more San Miguel, more snorting, and far fewer punchlines.

The Bird in Hand became our sanctuary. A pub that should've come with its own beds for us, considering how much time we spent there. I'd order pint after pint of San Miguel, always with that splash of lemonade like it made it less destructive somehow. We weren't drinking for the taste. We were drinking to fill silence. To laugh off our pain. To drown the parts of ourselves we didn't want to face.

But the real void? That lived in my pocket—in the form of dating apps.

Swiping became my new addiction. A way to feel wanted, even if it was by complete strangers. I paid for the upgrades—more likes, more matches, more meaningless validation. I'd sit at the pub bar, bored out of my skull, swiping like it was a job. Left, right, match, unmatch. Nothing ever stuck. Nothing ever felt real. But each ping of attention gave me a tiny hit of dopamine. Like a little pat on the back saying, "You're still wanted."

Ironically, in all that digital chaos, I reconnected with an ex. Of all people. And as strange as it was, it brought some weird kind of healing. We sat across from each other like two war vets comparing wounds, laughing at the madness, wondering how we even survived our pasts.

But the peace didn't last. It never did.

Substances became a constant. Cocaine, MDMA, anything to take the edge off—or ramp it up. Nights turned into mornings, mornings turned into regrets, and I was losing track of the version of myself I was pretending to be.

Then came the morning I met Ryan's future fiancée.

I shuffled into the living room, wrapped in a duvet like some sort of goblin who'd just emerged from a three-day cave rave. My toenails were an absolute disgrace—long enough to scratch through socks. She looked at them, then at me, and gave me that "what the actual fuck" look. Me, in all my impulsive glory, grabbed a pair of kitchen scissors and hacked at them right there on the couch. One of the clippings shot across the room like a rogue bullet. We never found it. Still haven't. But it became one of those stories we'll probably laugh about at my wedding—or funeral.

Not long after, I fell into another relationship. It started like they all did—intense, romantic, obsessive. She was older. Stable. I thought her stability might fix me. I moved in fast. I thought, "This is it. This is what I need."

Spoiler: it wasn't.

I showered her with gifts. Expensive perfume. Dinners. Trips. I bent over backwards trying to make her love me. But it wasn't love. It was fear. Fear of being alone. Fear of not being enough. I thought if I just gave enough, she'd stay. But beneath the surface, my insecurities bubbled. I snapped at small things.

The mask would slip, and I'd erupt—shouting, storming off, smashing glasses, slamming doors. Holidays didn't fix it. In fact, Mykonos became another warzone. Alcohol, sun, and my inability to handle emotion? A recipe for disaster. I still can't remember exactly what triggered that fight—but I know it ended with me crying in a bathroom, wondering what was wrong with me.

Then came Ibiza.

She went with her friend for a weekend. She told me she loved me. Promised she'd behave. That it was just drinks and sun and music. But I couldn't breathe. Every hour she didn't text back, I spiralled. My mind filled in the blanks—new guys, lies, betrayal. I didn't trust her. But really, I didn't trust myself to be enough.

So, I turned to what I knew. I sniffed. I lied. I coped the only way I'd taught myself how to—through destruction.

Things peaked one night when a mate came over for what was meant to be a quiet drink. A couple of pints. A chat. But by the time we got back to my girlfriend's flat, we were on MDMA. Quiet sniffing from a key, thinking we were subtle. We weren't. Her, my mum, and my sister were all in the house—and they'd seen us on the cameras.

She confronted me. I denied it. Badly. Then the rage took over. Embarrassed. Exposed. Cornered. I lashed out, verbally. Cruel, cutting words. I stormed out, jumped into my car, and drove like a maniac through the streets—not knowing where I was going, just knowing I had to get out. I didn't get far. Slammed into a curb. Blew out the tyre. Sat there in the dark, surrounded by glass and guilt, wondering what the hell I was doing with my life.

Eventually I wandered back to her place, only to find the police had come and gone. I didn't even have the decency to face them. I ran again. Slept at a mate's house like a coward.

But that wasn't the end.

The relationship collapsed under the weight of all my chaos. I ended it. Dramatically. Impulsively. I shattered picture frames, smashed memories, packed my life into bin bags and left. The police came. Again. It had become routine. A pattern.

I went back to my parents. Humbled. Broken. Lost. And, of course, I went straight to the pub. Because when your life is burning down, nothing soothes like a pint and pretending it doesn't hurt.

Around this time, I tried antidepressants for the first time. The GP wrote the prescription like they were handing out paracetamol. But the tablets didn't touch the root of it. They dulled the edge—but didn't kill the beast. I wasn't just depressed. I was unwell. But no one had put a name to it yet.

THE INVITATION TO THE DARKSIDE.

The days dragged. The weeks blurred. I was stuck in the same loop—drink, drugs, regret, repeat. I was hurting the people I loved. Hurting myself. But I

didn't know how to stop.

I wasn't in love. I wasn't healing. I was swiping through the void—hoping someone, something, anything would fill the hole I didn't know how to close.

It started like so many bad ideas do—with a line.

Just a casual search for cocaine. Nothing new. Nothing unexpected. But that night would mark the beginning of something much darker, something that would quietly, almost seductively, change the trajectory of my life. Not in one giant leap, but in little steps—one bump, one favour, one handshake at a time.

He wasn't your typical dealer. Not the twitchy, paranoid stereotype. No, this guy was smooth—charismatic, funny, well-dressed. A storyteller. The kind of bloke who could talk you into a fire and convince you it was a hot tub. His stories always came with flair—tales of exotic holidays, big business deals, crazy nights out, flashy cars. He had that aura, that look-at-me energy that made you want to be liked by him. And I did. That's how it started.

At first, we'd just chat when I picked up. A few jokes. A handshake. A bit of banter. He called me his "little brother." Always asked if I was alright, if I was "good for now." At the time, it felt like loyalty. Like someone actually gave a shit. But looking back, it was grooming, plain and simple. Not in the typical sense, but in the sense of building trust while slowly pulling you in.

The moment everything shifted was when he handed me a safe.

A small, black safe—nothing flashy. He asked if I could keep it in my loft. "Just for a bit, bro," he said casually, like it was a box of old DVDs. Inside it? The biggest amount of cocaine I had ever seen. Just sitting there above my head while I brushed my teeth or watched telly downstairs. I told myself I wasn't involved I was just holding it. A favour for a mate. But deep down, I knew. I was already neck deep.

He'd pop by, disappear into the loft, bag it up, hand me some for free. At first, it was exciting. Dangerous, yeah—but exciting. I had free coke, all the time. Unlimited supply. No one ever said it out loud, but it was clear: this was the beginning of something bigger. And I wanted in—because he liked me. And being liked, when you spend most of your life feeling like an outsider, is intoxicating.

Soon he started asking me to help.

Nothing major at first—just drop-offs when he was away. He gave me a burner phone that wouldn't stop ringing. I was driving around, collecting cash, handing over wraps, playing the role of someone, I never thought I'd become. All while he sipped cocktails in Spain. He was the boss. I was the runner. But I didn't care. I felt important. Connected. Seen.

And I was using constantly. The coke wasn't a reward anymore—it was just maintenance. I'd rack up massive tabs—£1,000 a week, easy. He'd come by, weigh what was left, and tell me what I owed. It wasn't even a conversation. And I paid, every time. Because what else could I do? Say no? He wasn't threatening—but he didn't need to be. The power imbalance was obvious. I was hooked. And he was my supplier, my mate, and my boss, all in one.

Then came Liverpool.

Late-night trips in my car. Backstreets. Dodgy estates. Cold alleyways and anonymous flats filled with shadowy figures and stale weed smoke. These weren't mates hanging out. This was business. Real business. Cash stacked in shoeboxes. Knives. Guns. Coke in kilos. People talking in code, checking windows, keeping lookouts. The kind of scenes you only see in films—until you're standing in one.

I kept my hands in my pockets. I didn't touch anything. I didn't speak unless spoken to. I knew my place. And every time we drove home in silence, my heart was hammering. I was carrying more drugs than I could explain in a million years. One blue light in the mirror and it was over. My life would be done. Prison. Headlines. My mum crying in a courtroom. That was the reality. But I kept going back. Because addiction doesn't think logically. It just thinks more.

I'd tell myself I wasn't like the others. That I wasn't really a dealer. That I was just helping out. But that's what every addict tells themselves when the line between user and mule gets blurry.

Eventually, I started saying no. Started stepping back. I'd seen too much. Knew too much. I wasn't cut out for that world. I could feel the danger closing in like a vice. I was one dodgy deal away from losing everything. But walking away wasn't clean.

He didn't like "no."

We'd been on holiday together just before COVID. During lockdown, we stayed in touch. Went on walks. Had little house sessions. He always made me feel like I was part of something. Until I owed him money. Then it was a different story. Then the smiles disappeared. The tone changed. And I realised—I was never his little brother. I was just a walking, talking bank account. My addiction was his business. And I'd made him rich.

He didn't have to do anything. I did it all. I ran the errands. Took the risks. Paid the debts. He sat back and counted the notes. And still, there was part of me that wanted his approval. That wanted to be seen as someone who belonged in his world.

But I didn't.

I wasn't built for it.

Not physically. Not mentally. Not emotionally. That world is fast and ruthless. And deep down, all I ever wanted was to feel safe. To feel loved. That's why I stayed as long as I did. Not for the money. Not even for the drugs. But for the feeling of mattering—even if it was fake.

Eventually, I walked away. Slowly. Quietly. I didn't make a scene. Just stopped picking up. Stopped dropping off. Stopped answering calls. I knew he could flip on me in a second. I knew I was disposable.

But I also knew I was done being someone else's pawn.

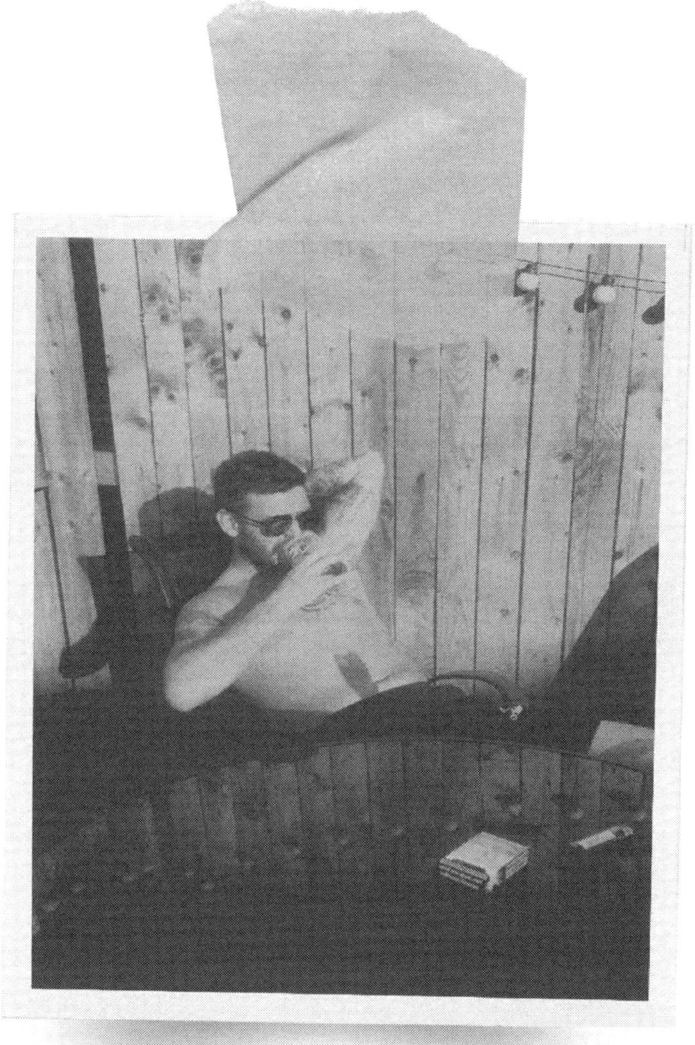

LOCKDOWN AND FALLOUT.

My phone buzzes – that little vibration that can either be the highlight of your day or the start of a right old mess. And this time? Oh, this time it was her. Name splashed across the screen, and my brain did a little double take. Hang on a minute… where do I know that cheeky glint in her eye from? It was like a half-formed memory, a proper brain fart moment. We start chatting, all casual like, and I blurt out,

"I swear I recognise you!"

Turns out, and get this for a plot twist, she was best mates with the girl. You know, the one I was supposed to, ahem, pop my cherry with back in the day? The one who, bless her heart, decided my lack of performance the night before was a dealbreaker. Charming, right?

So, here's her mate, years later, smiling at me from my bloody Tinder. Felt a bit like the universe was having a laugh, a proper cosmic nudge. The conversation? It just flowed, like we'd known each other for ages, a spark rekindled that I didn't even know was there in the first place. Then, BAM. The ex, bless her cotton socks, had apparently instructed her mate to ask the golden question:

"So, does his… thing work now?"

Cheers for that, love. Right in the feels, that did. Deeper than I'd care to admit, even though a part of me knew it was coming.

But for the record, yes it does.

A little bit too well, which brings even more annoyance.

My brain, bless its chaotic wiring thanks to the undiagnosed ADHD buzzing away in the background, probably hyper fixated on that possibility, making the anticipation even more of a bloody drama.

But despite that little gem of a question, the connection with this new girl? Electric. Proper puzzle pieces clicking into place. My brain, usually bouncing off the walls like a toddler on too much sugar, actually felt… calm. Focused. Which, looking back, was probably the novelty of the situation, the shiny new toy syndrome my ADHD brain loves. But life, as it always does, decided to chuck a spanner in the works.

She was a mum, her world revolving around her little girl and the wreckage of a past relationship. So, our time together? Snatched moments. Quick front door meets, after I finished work. Which felt like they were over in seconds, late-night texts that kept me buzzing like a faulty wire, hushed phone calls after bedtime.

Each stolen encounter left me wanting more, that limited time just amplifying the bloody_longing. My brain, naturally, would latch onto these moments, replaying them endlessly, the anticipation of the next meet-up becoming an all-consuming obsession. Classic ADHD, right? Intense focus on the new and exciting. But I was none the wiser to this little disorder my brain had just yet!

Then came Mexico.

Ah, Mexico.

A lads' holiday, a chance to hit the reset button, to forget the creeping anxiety about this weird virus everyone was whispering about. Little did we know, the world was about to go properly mental. Red wine, ice clinking in the glass by the pool, the sound of proper belly laughs echoing in the warm night air. And then she appeared.

Another one!

This time, a holiday romance, all playful smiles, and eyes that held the same fiery glow as those bloody amazing sunsets we watched together. She was older. Older than my mum. Proper grown-up vibes, but with this incredible youthful energy. It was intense, passionate, the kind of whirlwind affair that's perfectly designed for a holiday, confined to the golden sand and the ridiculously blue sea. My brain, completely overstimulated by the new environment, the excitement, the novelty of a new person, was in its element. The impulsivity, the seeking of intense experiences.

But paradise, as always, had an expiry date.

Back home I came, this weird fatigue clinging to me like a damp towel. A cough that rattled my chest so hard I was literally gasping for air, and my body ached in places I didn't even know existed. The news was full of this "novel virus" chat, a mysterious illness spreading like wildfire.

Looking back now?

I'm almost certain I was one of the unlucky sods who got it early. My body felt like it was trying to fight off an alien invasion, and my brain, foggy and overwhelmed, just wanted to curl up and hide.

Despite feeling like I'd been run over by a truck, I knew I had to deal with the absolute mess my love life had become. The distance, the age gap, the reality of life back home – it all felt like climbing Mount Everest in flip-flops with the older woman.

So, we said our goodbyes. Bittersweet doesn't even cover it. A weird mix of guilt for ending something that felt so intense, and relief that I didn't have to navigate that complicated reality anymore. My brain, unknowingly, was always seeking the next dopamine hit, was probably already subconsciously moving on, even as a part of me felt a slight bit of sadness. Then I messaged the girl from Tinder again.

A proper dick move, but I couldn't stop thinking about her.

Her easy smile, her unwavering support, became my anchor in the brewing storm. As the world went into lockdown, that proper, everyone-panic-buying-toilet-roll kind of lockdown, fear and uncertainty were hanging in the air like a bad smell. We made a snap decision, fuelled by a desperate need for connection and that shared vulnerability that comes with facing the unknown. Basically, we moved in together.

Well, sort of.

We had to work around when her daughter was with her dad, it was way too soon to introduce me to that part of her life. My impulsive nature probably played a big part in that quick decision. The idea of companionship, of not being alone in this terrifying new reality, was incredibly appealing to my easily overwhelmed brain.

But the initial excitement of living together soon morphed into the bloody monotony of isolation. The four walls of the house started to feel like they were closing in, the days blurring into an endless loop of Netflix and Deliveroo. The weight of the pandemic pressed down on us, a constant, low-level hum of anxiety. My brain deprived of its usual stimulation, started to get properly agitated.

Alcohol became more of a crutch, a way to numb the fear and the boredom. And then cocaine, that slippery snake, slithered back into my life. But this time, it wasn't a bite. It had its body wrapped around me, constricting me.

It started as a weekend thing, a way to break the soul-crushing routine. But, as it always does, the line blurred. The white powder offered this fake sense of control, a temporary escape from the chaos outside and a way to make the endless hours tick by faster. It was a bloody dangerous spiral, and I was hurtling downwards. The impulsivity, the seeking of immediate gratification was practically throwing a party. The consequences? My brain wasn't even registering them in the short term.

Then, one random afternoon, acting purely on impulse (surprise, surprise), I messaged some lady selling kittens. Saw this little grey fluffball and, bam, that afternoon he was home. Kenny. A proper furry little agent of chaos in our already chaotic world. His playful antics, his sudden bursts of energy, brought this much-needed shot of joy into our lockdown existence. At night, he'd curl up on my chest, this purring little reminder of simpler times. The novelty of a pet, the constant movement and interaction, was probably a welcome distraction.

But even Kenny's adorable face couldn't completely dispel the dark cloud hanging over our relationship – her ex. The father of her daughter. Proper master manipulator, that bloke. A narcissist who used their kid like a bloody weapon. Bombarding her with calls and messages, full of accusations and threats. Painting me as the big bad wolf.

I mean I can be, but it was like my alter ego, I never actually wanted to let out!

Even though they were separated, his controlling grip was still tight, his presence a constant source of stress for both of us. My heightened sensitivity to perceived threats and injustices, made me absolutely seethe with anger at this bloke's behaviour.

As restrictions started to ease, we were desperate for some bloody normalcy. A day trip to Thorpe Park with her mate and her boyfriend seemed like the perfect escape. But the night before?

Disaster.

Fuelled by booze and simmering tensions, I just erupted. A proper drunken rage. Jealousy, insecurity, the lingering effects of the cocaine or the fact we were in another part of the country and couldn't get any – it all just bubbled over. I became a spectacle, a walking, talking explosion of my own inner turmoil. The shame and remorse that followed?

Crippling.

But the damage was done. We still went to Thorpe Park, to a degree. But understandably, she needed space. Didn't know how to deal with my… outbursts. We made up, things were good again. For a bit. My emotional dysregulation, meant my reactions could be disproportionate and intense, often leaving me feeling immense guilt afterwards.

The final, tragic act of our little play unfolded the night before Christmas Eve. My usual sources for the nose candy had gone quiet, the festive season messing with the supply chain. She knew how desperate I was, so she mentioned a connection. An ex-lover.

Someone who could sort us out, but...

"I wasn't going to like who it was".

A proper wave of jealousy hit me; my insecurities amplified by the craving. Being drunk, and then remembering her saying, right at the start of our relationship, that

"he's the only person who's ever made her finish" during sex?

This phantom rival had become a bloody obsession. Who was he? What was he like? Was he everything I wasn't? My brain, fixated on this one detail, spiralled into a pit of paranoia and self-doubt.

The night just went completely mental. A proper maelstrom of accusations and paranoia. Fuelled by alcohol, the desperate need for cocaine, and my own self-destructive tendencies, I tore through her house in a blind rage. Holes punched in walls, tablets smashed, the remnants of our life together scattered across the floor like confetti at a funeral.

Utter devastation. A physical representation of the absolute chaos inside my head. My impulsivity, the inability to regulate my emotions, the desperate need to lash out as I didn't know how to deal with the feelings I was feeling inside – it was all there, a horrifying display of my inner demons.

The inevitable and well-deserved arrest followed.

Cold cell, the harsh reality of my actions sinking in like a stone. Our relationship, like so many before, had ended in the same bloody destruction. The shattered pieces of our bond lay amongst the wreckage of that night.

Bail. Conditions: stay away from her house, no contact until a certain date. That month was hell. Pure, unadulterated hell. Remorse, guilt, the desperate need for her to understand that those thirty minutes of madness didn't define who I was. I went sober the day I got out of that cell. Knew, deep down, that booze and drugs were massive fuel for those explosions. Even if I didn't understand my own brain still.

A month later, a letter. Poured my heart out, all my regret and apology crammed onto those pages. I knew I'd messed up, spectacularly.

But her mate?

She twisted it. Saw only a selfish plea, completely devoid of any real remorse.

"You're making this all about you," she said, her words a proper knife twist. I knew her friend was poisoning the well, manipulating her pain for her own twisted kicks. I get it, right? If your mates with someone capable of that, you'd try and steer them clear. But that wasn't the real me. It was in me, yeah, that darkness. But I was trying so hard to understand why, how it happened.

We never really spoke again. The ghost of us lingered, a proper haunting reminder of a love lost in the madness of the pandemic and the bloody mess inside my own head. The guilt, the regret?

They still gnaw away at me. A constant reminder of my own self-destruction.

She became this bittersweet memory, a love forever tainted by the events of that bloody awful year.

I didn't just walk away from this relationships and others in my past with a broken heart – I walked away believing I was unlovable. That I was too much, too intense, too hard to deal with. Their words echoed in my head for years. Every argument became proof that I was the problem. I kept shrinking myself down, masking who I was just to try and be accepted – even if it meant losing myself in the process.

THE LOCKDOWN SESSIONS.

The world outside had gone silent.

The streets, once pulsing with life, now stood empty—like veins stripped of blood. Shops were boarded up like forgotten windows in an abandoned town. Even the birds seemed to sing more quietly. The air carried a weight, thick with dread and static, like something big was coming... or had already arrived.

Lockdown didn't just change our routines—it rewrote reality. And while everyone else seemed to settle into banana bread and Joe Wicks workouts, I was slipping into something very different.

It began, as most things do, with a text.

"Fancy a few beers at mine tonight? Low-key. Just a couple of us in the back garden." - Simon.

A mate from the local. Loud. Magnetic. The kind of laugh you could hear three streets over. You always knew when Simon was in the room—and you were always glad he was. We'd both been part of the regulars' furniture at the Bird in Hand before it shut down. Now, here he was, offering a brief taste of the world we'd lost.

At that point, I was staying in my nan's empty house. My parents were high-risk, and I was still working, classed as a "key worker," which gave me just enough freedom to feel both lucky and cursed. I was climbing the walls. The thought of human interaction—actual laughter, not filtered through a screen—was too tempting to ignore.

That night, after a couple of beers in the garden, we drifted inside. One by one, our barriers lowered with every drink. The curtains were drawn. Music, not loud, but loud enough to feel something, filled the space. Jokes bounced around. The smell of stale ale mixed with rolling tobacco. It felt... illegal. Because it was. But it also felt like a lifeline. Like air rushing into lungs that had been starved of connection.

The COVID bar was born.

It didn't take long for word to get around. The pub may have been shut, but we had something even better—a secret sanctuary. Every weekend, and sometimes midweek if boredom hit hard enough, Simon's place transformed. We were a rotating crew: familiar faces from the pub, a few neighbours, the occasional stranger who just happened to know the right dog walker. If you were in, you were in. It was hush-hush, phones away, no stories posted. What happened at Simon's stayed at Simon's.

And in that living room, something powerful happened.

Yes, there were pints. Yes, there were bags of coke. But there was also something else—something raw and human. We weren't just escaping lockdown. We were reclaiming ourselves. We laughed harder, danced like idiots in that tiny space, cried when the mood turned. We toasted birthdays and mourned those we'd lost. We shared fears that we couldn't say out loud anywhere else.

There was something tribal about it. Defiant. Sacred, even.

We were breaking rules, and we knew it. The guilt came in waves—especially when you remembered the people really suffering out there. But in those moments, when the music dropped and your best mate handed you a drink, it was easy to justify. We needed this. We needed each other.

There were nights when paranoia crept in. A police car driving past sent everyone ducking. The front room would fall silent in an instant, only for someone to whisper, "We're good," and the noise would start up again. We lived on that edge—half guilty, half euphoric. And it was addictive.

Cocaine, always the silent companion, started to lace more of our nights. It wasn't about getting wired—it was about stretching the moment. Making time last longer. Anything to delay the return to that grey, quiet world outside.

But even with all the madness, the lockdown sessions weren't about the drugs. Not really.

They were about connection.

In a time where we were told to isolate, we found each other. We created a family, bound not by blood but by survival. In that house, with its dim lights and stacked beer cans, we could breathe again. Be ourselves again. Be human again.

And no one embodied that spirit more than Simon.

He was the glue. The heartbeat. The one who always made sure the fridge was stocked, the ashtray was emptied, and the vibes were high. He didn't care who you were—if you needed a laugh, a drink, or a rant, he had time for you. No judgement. Just kindness, with a side of chaos.

Simon didn't want fuss. Ever. Even when life kicked him in the teeth, he still found a way to smile. To make you laugh even when you didn't want to. He brought people together in a time when everything else was pulling us apart.

He passed away while I was writing this chapter.

And truthfully, I still can't wrap my head around it. Because how can someone that alive just be... gone?

That one is for you, mate.

For every time you topped up my pint without asking. For every time you made a dark day lighter. For every laugh, every nod across the room, every time you said, "come on, it's only a quick one" and it turned into 3am.

You were the best of us. And this chapter—this mad, beautiful, rebellious chapter—was only what it was, because of you.

Miss You Brother!

I love you, mate. I always will.

Rest easy.

THE AFTERMATH AND NEW BEGINNINGS.

The wreckage of my ex's house mirrored the wreckage within me. The arrest, the shame, the crushing weight of my actions – it all culminated in a period of profound darkness. I moved back in with my parents, the prodigal son returning with his tail between his legs, vowing to leave alcohol behind for good.

After months of wallowing in self-pity, I sought solace in the familiar escape of dating apps. It was there, amidst the endless swiping and superficial profiles, that I stumbled upon a new girl. It was on Bumble, an app which had the girl messaging the boy first, a sort of role reversal that suited my bruised ego and low self-confidence. Our first date was a walk around her village, a COVID-compliant alternative to the usual pub or restaurant setting. We talked for hours, the miles melting away as we connected on a deeper level.

She felt like a breath of fresh air, a beacon of light in the darkness that had consumed me. I quickly moved into hers, staying there more than my parents' house, which offered little comfort or escape from my own thoughts. Driven by a need for change and a desire to build a new life, I began searching for a house of my own. Impulsively, perhaps recklessly, I purchased a four-bedroom detached house, a space far larger than my needs required.

My now girlfriend's family were big drinkers. Wine flowed freely at every gathering, and the temptation eventually wore me down. What started as a social lubricant soon morphed into a nightly ritual. The alcohol numbed the pain, the guilt, the ever-present anxiety.

She began taking charge of how to furnish the house. Not wanting to upset or disappoint her, I agreed to things that weren't to my taste. Even her own sister told her to stop taking over and let me enjoy the process, but I sided with my girlfriend anyway. The excitement of the purchase was fleeting. Once the keys were in my hand and the reality of my solitary existence set in, a wave of depression washed over me. The ADHD, always lurking beneath the surface, amplified the feelings of emptiness and lack of direction. The house, once a symbol of hope, became a monument to my loneliness.

Secretly, I continued to use cocaine. Every time my girlfriend went to visit her parents, I would feign a migraine, retreating into the shadows of my own home. Days would blur into a haze of cocaine-fuelled isolation, the guilt and shame compounding with each passing hour. When she eventually moved in, this brought a semblance of stability.

We welcomed Otto, an adorable golden retriever puppy, into our lives. I remember wanting to get him as quickly as I could, spending lots of time travelling to see him before he was old enough to bring home. We brought him home on New Year's Eve. He quickly became my lifeline, my furry companion who demanded walks, playtime, and unconditional love. Otto forced me out of my self-imposed isolation, dragging me into nature and reminding me of the simple joys in life.

Prior to getting the keys to my house, it was my girlfriend who first suggested I might have ADHD. My struggles with focus, impulsivity, addictions, and emotional regulation were becoming increasingly apparent. After some extensive research, or what I call going down the rabbit hole, I sought a private diagnosis, and the confirmation brought a strange mix of relief and grief. Relief that there was an explanation for my lifelong struggles, grief for the life I could have had with earlier intervention.

The diagnosis was a catalyst for change. Medication helped to manage the symptoms, but it was the internal shift that truly made the difference. I embarked on a journey of self-discovery, learning about my neurodiversity and embracing the unique strengths and challenges it presented.

However, she struggled to understand. She didn't believe in mental health issues, a red flag I perhaps shouldn't have ignored. Her initial reaction was one of disappointment and frustration. "We can't have a baby until you sort your head out," she said, her words laced with judgment and impatience. My hyperfocus on understanding ADHD became a source of contention. "You've become more ADHD since your diagnosis," she'd complain, expressing a preference for the "old me," the one who was less self-aware and more easily controlled.

My old BMW, a car I adored, was a constant source of derision for her. "It's so old," she'd sneer. I now think her disdain for my car was just another way to undermine my confidence. Then came the Mercedes. A gleaming white E450, a £50,000 symbol of her success and ambition. I agreed to let her finance my car and get rid of the BMW.

With her away on a work trip, I cared for Otto and also embarked on a garden transformation. Days blurred into physical labour as a friend and I stripped the garden, laid paving slabs, constructed decking, and rolled out fake grass. Each night, fuelled by cocaine and beer, I pushed my body to its limits. Each morning knowing I needed sleep; I would combine sleeping tablets with the drugs already in my system. One morning, I didn't wake up. My friend broke down the door, fearing the worst.

When my girlfriend called from Mauritius, her concern was solely focused on Otto's well-being. Upon her return, the newly transformed garden was met with indifference. A diagnosis of skin cancer further strained our relationship. I had used sunbeds and tanning injections since Mexico, and the cancerous lesion was the result. The day I had it removed, she barely acknowledged it. Her excuse: "I'm sorry, my boss has been crying."

The realization that we weren't meant to be, hit me one sleepless night. I went for a long drive and confessed upon returning that we should split up. The next morning, I returned home from work to an empty house. Otto and all her belongings were gone.

The days that followed were a blur of grief and confusion. I mourned the loss of the relationship, the loss of the home I had built, and most of all, the loss of Otto. The ADHD diagnosis had become a burden. I felt like a fraud. My drinking escalated. Cocaine became my constant companion again. I would often find myself drinking alone, the silence of the empty house amplifying my loneliness.

The paranoid thoughts consumed my mind. More times than I can count, I was convinced people were going to raid my house. I was slipping again, sinking back into that same self-destructive cycle I had promised myself I would never return to.

But something had changed. This time, I had awareness. This time, I had tools. I just needed to find the strength to use them.

STEPPING INTO THE RING.

The silence in the house wasn't just a lack of noise—it was a weight. A heaviness that settled into the floorboards, the furniture, my chest. The emptiness after my ex left, taking Otto with her, felt physical. I'd lost the dog I adored, the partner I'd tried to build a future with, and even the illusion that love, on its own, was enough to fix what was broken inside me.

I was tired. Tired of being angry. Tired of ruining things. Tired of being tired.

But buried underneath that exhaustion was a flicker of something else. Not hope—something more primal. Rage. Restlessness. I wasn't just trying to outrun my past anymore—I wanted to confront it. Head-on. I needed something to channel the chaos, or I'd combust.

That's when I made the most unexpected decision of my life: I signed up for a white-collar boxing match.

To anyone who knew me, it sounded like a joke. Me? The guy who'd spent years avoiding conflict? The one who'd internalised every slight until it exploded in all the wrong ways? The guy who'd rather disappear than confront someone face to face? I wasn't the type to pick fights—I was the type to implode from the inside out.

But maybe that's why it made sense. I didn't want to fight other people. I needed to fight myself—the version of me that kept destroying everything good. The version of me that didn't believe I could ever change.

I found a local gym—raw, loud, and dripping in sweat. No polished machines or plush towels. Just grit. I walked in and immediately felt like I didn't belong. But I stayed. I signed the waiver. I wrapped my hands. I got in the ring.

My first sparring session was a reality check I didn't ask for. I was paired with someone clearly more experienced. He moved like water. I moved like someone trying to punch a wasp. Every jab he landed felt personal. He danced around me while I flailed and froze. At one point, I turned away, hands up, like a kid getting caught stealing sweets. Embarrassing doesn't even begin to cover it.

By the end of that round, I wasn't just battered I was humiliated. I left the gym that day deflated, ashamed, convinced I'd made a mistake.

But something weird happened when I got home. I didn't wallow. I didn't open a bottle or message a dealer. I picked up the phone and called a friend.

He said something simple, but it stuck: "Good. You needed that. That's your baseline. Now build from it."

So, I did.

I trained. Harder than I ever had at anything. Day after day. I watched my punches get sharper. My body getting leaner. My confidence inch forward. Each bruise became a badge of progress. I started to see myself differently—not as the angry guy who lost control, but as someone who could focus. Who could grind. Who could show up for himself.

And something shifted. I stopped drinking altogether. No more weekend sessions. No more pretending the coke made me social when it just numbed the shame. For the first time in years, I had a reason not to escape my mind—I had a reason to sharpen it.

Then came the body shot.

One perfectly placed punch in sparring took the wind out of me—literally. I dropped like a sack of bricks, gasping for breath, chest on fire. At first, I thought it was just bruised ribs. But the pain stuck around. A hospital scan showed a blood clot in my lung. Life-threatening. My fight had to be postponed.

It felt like the universe kicking me in the teeth just as I was getting up. But weirdly, I didn't spiral. I rested. Recovered. Stayed off the drink. I kept visualising that fight. That ring. That walk through the crowd.

When I finally got cleared to train again, I came back sharper—mentally and physically. And when fight night finally arrived, I was ready.

Walking into the venue, I felt the nerves kick in. My legs went to jelly. My stomach churned. I was about to fight in front of hundreds of people, most of whom didn't even know my name. The lights, the noise, the smell of sweat and adrenaline—it was overwhelming. But I kept moving forward. I stepped into the ring.

It felt like everything around me disappeared. No crowd. No ex. No broken furniture. No Otto. Just me, my opponent, and the bell.

Round one. I took some hits. Gave some back. Found my rhythm. I'd trained too hard to let fear win now.

Round two. My lungs were burning, but I stayed focused. This wasn't about winning. It was about not giving up on myself.

Round three. I fought like hell. The final bell rang. I didn't collapse. I stood tall.

The judges gave the win to my opponent. Some said it was controversial. But honestly, I didn't care.

Because I'd already won.

I'd stepped into that ring as a man trying to escape the ghosts of his past—and I walked out a fighter. I raised thousands for Cancer Research UK. I walked out sober. Clean. Focused. I didn't need validation. I didn't need revenge.

I just needed to know I was capable of change.

I found out that night that I was.

AWAKENING TO THE UNIVERSE.

Boxing taught me how to take a hit—but what it really gave me was a chance to listen. Not just to my coach barking instructions, not just to the thud of gloves hitting pads. I mean really listen. To myself. To the silence between the noise. To something deeper I couldn't yet explain.

After the fight, something in me had shifted. I was off alcohol. I was clean. My body felt stronger, but my mind… it was reaching for something more. I'd pushed through pain, fear, and setbacks, and somewhere along that brutal, bloody journey, I'd opened a door I hadn't known was even there. It wasn't just about the fight anymore. I'd sparked something spiritual—and I couldn't ignore it.

It started with numbers. Weird ones. Repeating ones. 11:11 on the microwave clock. 222 on a car plate. 333 on a takeaway receipt. At first, I laughed it off. Coincidence. Just my brain pattern-matching. But when you keep seeing the same numbers repeatedly—when it follows you from petrol stations to phone battery percentages—it stops being funny and starts feeling like something else.

Curious (and with the usual ADHD hyperfocus kicking in), I started digging. I read about "angel numbers." Spiritual breadcrumbs, little nudges from the universe. 1111 was new beginnings. 222 meant trust the process. 333 meant the universe had your back.

It sounded mad. But it felt real.

This led me down another rabbit hole: The Law of Attraction. I read The Secret. Then The Key. I watched videos, listened to podcasts, journaled like a man possessed. The idea that our thoughts create our reality. That what we focus on, we attract? It was like someone had handed me a manual for the chaos that had ruled my life for years.

The more I read, the more it made sense. I'd been unconsciously manifesting disaster—feeding my insecurities with fear and anger, attracting pain because pain was all I believed I deserved. But what if I could change that? What if I was in control?

It wasn't about being delusional or ignoring the hard stuff. It was about gratitude. Focus. Clarity. About tuning into the present, even when the present was hard.

I started small.

Gratitude every morning. Three things. No matter how shit the day before had been. A warm brew. A cuddle from the cats. Clean sheets. The smell of grass after it rains. Simple. Grounding. Real.

Then I started visualising. Properly. Feeling what it would be like to live the life I wanted. Not just imagine it, but feel it—peace, purpose, love, contentment. I spoke affirmations out loud, even when I felt stupid: I am worthy. I am safe. I am changing. Slowly, my inner voice—the one that had spent years tearing me down—started getting drowned out by something softer. Kinder.

And the synchronicities? They kept coming. I'd think about an old friend, and they'd message me. I'd worry about something, then get unexpected, good news the next day. I'd hear a song on the radio that echoed exactly what I'd been feeling. The universe was responding. Not always with fireworks, but with quiet, undeniable signs.

It wasn't about religion. It wasn't about some cosmic genie granting wishes. It was about connection. Awareness. Energy. Realising that I wasn't alone and never had been.

When I started trusting life instead of trying to wrestle it into submission, things shifted. I stopped catastrophising every worst-case scenario. I stopped chasing people who didn't want to be caught. I started allowing—letting go of the need to control everything. Trusting that what's meant for me will find me. That if I do the inner work, the outer stuff will follow.

Some days were hard. Doubt still crept in. Old thought patterns tried to reclaim space in my mind. But now, I had tools. Breathing deeply. Sitting with my emotions instead of suppressing them. Walking in nature without headphones. Journaling. Pausing instead of reacting. I wasn't perfect—but I was present.

The more positive energy I put out, the more positive experiences I welcomed. I wasn't just reacting to life anymore—I was co-creating it. And that gave me something I hadn't felt in a long time: power.

True power. The kind that doesn't come from dominance or bravado, but from knowing who you are—even when the world doesn't quite understand you yet.

The universe isn't loud. It doesn't scream. It whispers. You just have to be still long enough to hear it.

For the first time in my life, I was listening.

THE BOYS.

The silence that filled the house after my ex left with Otto was unlike anything I'd ever felt before. Not the peaceful kind of silence you get after a long day, but the kind that crawls under your skin and weighs down your chest. The rooms echoed with absence. Her perfume still lingered in the air. Otto's fur still clung to the corners of the couch. Their energy was gone, but the memories were everywhere. I'd lost a partner and a companion in one swift blow, and what remained was a crushing loneliness I didn't know what to do with.

I remembered a conversation with my ex when things were still relatively good—when we'd laugh in bed and imagine a future that now felt like a distant memory. "What would you do if we broke up and I took the dog?" she asked one night, probably thinking nothing of it. I didn't either, at the time. I joked, "I'd get a cat." But now I was living the reality of that hypothetical, and it didn't feel like a joke anymore. The loneliness hit hard.

True to form, my impulsivity took over. I started browsing local listings for kittens, not really thinking it through—just reacting, trying to fill a void the same way I always had fast, emotionally, and without a plan. I told myself I just needed one. A little companion to curl up on the sofa with me during the long evenings when the silence became too much.

I found a litter of Maine Coon crosses nearby. When I arrived, I was instantly drawn to one of them. A chunky little guy, twice the size of his siblings, bold as anything, with a playful look in his eye. The woman selling him had nicknamed him "Big G." I was going to name him Bugzy, after Bugzy Malone, one of my favourite UK rappers. But as I sat watching him play, it hit me—he needed a sidekick.

"Do you have another one left?" I asked.

She did. A tabby, slightly more reserved, soulful eyes, slower to trust. But there was no denying the bond between the two. They were brothers. They wrestled together, slept together, played together. The thought of separating them felt wrong, like tearing apart something pure. So, in true impulsive fashion—and already £800 lighter thanks to a rushed credit card cash withdrawal—I brought them both home.

I named them Ronnie and Reggie, after the Kray twins. It just made sense. Two brothers. Mischievous, loyal, and a little chaotic. Ronnie was the bold one at first—curious, always exploring. Reggie was cautious, watchful, always hanging back before following his brother's lead. But as time went on, they flipped. Reggie became the brave one, Ronnie more reserved. Just like people, animals grow into their own personalities.

Driving home with two tiny kittens mewing in the passenger seat, I felt a rush of emotions. Responsibility. Hope. Doubt. Could I really care for them properly? I could barely manage my own emotions half the time. But I had to try. They deserved more than a broken man with an empty house.

I converted the kitchen into a safe space for them. Comfy bedding, toys scattered across the floor, a second-hand sofa I dragged in just so I could sleep close to them the first few weeks. I didn't want them to feel abandoned like I did. And slowly, they began to settle in. The once-quiet house started to buzz with life again—the sound of paws skidding across the tiles, tiny meows at breakfast, the odd crash of something being knocked over.

They followed me everywhere. To the bathroom, the garden, the office. When I worked, they curled up beside my laptop. When I paced around in one of my ADHD spirals, they watched quietly, occasionally brushing against my legs as if to say, "We're here."

They saw it all—my highs, my crashes, my chaotic creative bursts, and my self-destructive lows. They saw me at my worst. During my cocaine binges, when the paranoia took over and I locked them in the kitchen while I spiralled in the office, they waited. Every single time, without fail, when the sun came up and shame took over, they greeted me with head bumps and purrs. No judgement. Just love. Just presence.

Ronnie and Reggie weren't just pets—they were my reset button. When I lost myself, they brought me back.

Of course, it wasn't all smooth sailing. I tried to make the garden escape-proof, building what I thought was a solid perimeter. I underestimated just how determined two Maine Coon crosses could be. Within a day, they were on the roof of the shed. I resorted to Air Tags, attaching them to their collars like a paranoid parent, tracking their every move through the neighbourhood.

I remember sprinting through the estate in my slippers, climbing over fences, pushing through bushes with cuts on my arms just to find them. At one point, they made it into the nearby building site. I scaled a pile of bricks and found Reggie calmly sitting on top, watching the sunset like he hadn't caused a panic attack.

I even tried to fit a cat flap myself. I'd watched three YouTube videos and decided I was suddenly a glazier. One shattered double-glazed panel and a bruised ego later, I gave up and called in a professional. Still, I tried.

They were chaos. But they were mine.

They brought out a side of me I'd buried—softness, patience, nurture. They reminded me how good it felt to take care of something other than myself. They gave me structure. They gave me company when I couldn't bear to speak to another human being. And slowly, they helped me stitch a bit of myself back together.

Ronnie and Reggie didn't fix me. But they filled a space that I thought would stay empty forever. They made my house a home again. They made the silence bearable. And even now, when I'm pacing in my head or talking to myself in the mirror, they just look up at me like, "He's doing it again," then go back to sleep.

And if that's not unconditional love, I don't know what is.

THE BIRTH OF ATTENTIVE.

The seeds of Attentive Apparel were planted in the quiet chaos of rejection. It didn't sprout from a business plan or a boardroom brainstorm—it bloomed from frustration, a gut-punch moment that would spark a mission. I was lying in bed next to my Ex, the kind of late-night stillness where thoughts run wild. I'd been spiralling in deep thought about my recent ADHD diagnosis, and for once, the endless stream of ideas didn't feel like noise. It felt like purpose.

"I want to start a clothing brand," I told her.

She didn't even lift her head from her phone. "We've got more important things to pay for," she replied flatly, barely acknowledging the excitement in my voice.

In that moment, I knew two things: first, she didn't believe in me. Second, I had to do it anyway. Her words stung, not because she doubted the business, but because she doubted me. That kind of dismissal wasn't new—it was a recurring theme. Any time I wanted to break the mould or step into something outside the box, I was met with resistance.

But this time, her disapproval ignited something in me. If anything, it gave me the fuel I needed. I wasn't doing it despite her—I was doing it because of her. Because I'd spent too long dimming my light to keep others comfortable.

Soon after, the relationship ended. Right on cue, the 11:11s started showing up everywhere. On clocks, receipts, car registrations. To many it might've meant nothing, but to me, those numbers were my own personal signal—new beginnings, alignment, spiritual nudges. It felt like the universe was whispering, "Now's the time."

The hyperfocus kicked in. The kind only those with ADHD will understand. I became obsessed—in the best way. I threw myself into boxing training and building the brand. I was working overnight shifts, boxing in the evenings, and staying up through the early hours sketching logo ideas, reading about materials, researching screen printing.

The original name? Attentive Clothing. I registered the name at 3 a.m. during a night shift. I didn't have a solid plan. No investor, no market research, no spreadsheet with projections. What I did have was vision—and a reason. And sometimes, that's all you need.

I designed the first logo myself. I knew it had to represent attention, awareness, and the duality of neurodivergence. I scoured suppliers for weeks. Tried samples. Wore them. Washed them. Slept in them. Sent them to mates to get their honest opinions. When I found the hoodie—the one with weight in the fabric, enough room to breathe, and a silhouette that felt right—I knew I had my flagship piece.

The sensory-weighted hoodie took off almost immediately. It wasn't just a hoodie. It became a symbol. Of being seen, of comfort, of identity. Neurodivergent people finally had a piece of clothing made for them, not just marketed to them.

Social media became my outlet. I started posting videos explaining my diagnosis, showing how ADHD shows up in everyday life, and sharing the story behind the brand. People related. Not just locally—but globally. Messages started pouring in from parents of ADHD kids, late-diagnosed adults, people who said for the first time they felt understood.

The community began to build itself. People like Chris from (@happinessinmovement)—a guy I used to watch on TikTok and relate to without ever speaking to him. Now, he's a mate. Someone who gets it. Then there was Nush (@neuronush), a powerhouse on social media and an absolute legend when it comes to supporting the brand. She not only helped grow awareness but made the ADHD space feel inclusive and informed.

I connected with Beth (@livingwith.adhd_), a fellow Chester native, who helped with early photoshoots and became another grounding person in the whirlwind. Greg (@ADHGreg) lent support through honest convos and constant encouragement. There was also Daryl from @a.d.h.delicious_kitchen—a chef with ADHD who, true to his name, makes delicious food and has backed Attentive from day one.

Even Joe Foster, the founder of Reebok, got involved. Not only did he buy the hoodie and wear it proudly—he also offered his time, support, and guidance as a mentor. Imagine the founder of Reebok saying your idea is solid. That was one of those pinch-me moments.

Then came podcast invitations. I shared my story on MenTalkHealth with Ed and Matt. I sat down with Lauren Jennings (@the_adhd_queen), Miss Essex 2024. I chatted with Finty Bateman from Bad B With ADHD. Each time, the nerves were there. But with every conversation, the anxiety chipped away. I started to understand that sharing my experience was the brand. People weren't just buying clothes—they were buying into connection, into truth.

Attentive Apparel was never about fashion. It was about recognition. So that someone with ADHD or autism could clock someone else wearing it and go, "They get it." That little nod of mutual understanding.

But building a brand while battling your own demons is no joke. The highs? Unmatched. That rush when someone buys your product and messages you saying it helped them. That's what keeps you going. But the lows hit hard too. Behind the scenes, I was juggling debt, maxed-out credit cards, and working extra hours to stay afloat. Over £50,000 in personal debt, slowly chipped away through a management plan. It was all or nothing.

And then there was cocaine.

Even as the business grew, the addiction still whispered in my ear. I wasn't doing it every day, but when the pressure piled on, I'd cave. Some nights I'd be up doing orders and replying to emails, all while battling comedowns and anxiety. I'd use to silence the noise, to escape the burnout. It wasn't sustainable, and I knew it. But it's hard to step away when it feels like your only outlet.

Still, I kept going. Because Attentive wasn't just my business—it was my therapy, my purpose, my way out. It gave me structure. It gave me a reason to get out of bed. It reminded me that even on the worst days, someone out there was wearing my hoodie and feeling a little less alone.

Looking back, I realise that rejection from my Ex was one of the best things that could have happened. Her "no" was the catalyst for my "yes." Her doubt gave birth to belief. And now, the brand that was born in a dark bedroom, from a misunderstood diagnosis and a spark of defiance, has become something so much bigger than me.

Attentive is a movement. A message. A mission. And it's only just getting started, with or without the apparel side.

Other Influencers and supporters of Attentive Apparel worth a follow and who I'm immensely proud of also!

Molly Brooks-Dridge (**@mollys_adhd_mayhem)**

Emma Llewellyn (@**emmasmindovermatter)**

Sarah Dickinson (@**adhd.khaleesi**)

Nicola Burls (@**nikki_burls)**

Priyanka (**@littlemiss_adhd**)

Charlotte Ashley (**@charlotte_ashleyfitness**)

Claire Michalski (**@modernhippiemindset)**

Geraldine Kotstrewa (**@cherry. adhd**)

Amie Barlow (**@_amiebarlow**)

THE TIKTOK TRIGGER.

My newfound confidence, fuelled by boxing training and a spiritual awakening, had started bleeding into every part of my life—especially online. I started uploading workout clips and honest thoughts on TikTok. At first, it was just about keeping myself accountable, but it quickly became a way to express my recovery and promote the message behind Attentive Apparel.

It was in this digital storm of dopamine, dance trends, and duets that I stumbled across someone who would quietly detonate a new chapter in my emotional chaos.

And then, BAM! On Halloween - A comment. Simple enough, just a "keep going" type thing about my efforts training in my garage gym. But something about her profile… it just clicked. Seemed like she was on a similar "level up your life" mission. So, naturally, I did a bit of digging. And by digging, I looked at her profile picture. And then the DMs started flying. Instant connection, proper rapid-fire stuff. Deep chats about dreams, the kind of vulnerabilities you usually only share with your therapist (or your cats), and this weird sense of "have we met before in a past life or something?"

My brain, always on the lookout for novelty and intense connection, was absolutely buzzing. This was interesting.

Turns out, timing is a funny old thing. I was crawling out of my own personal pit of despair, all shiny and new with my rediscovered mojo, I was so sure I wasn't looking for anything though!

She, on the other hand, was navigating the choppy waters of a separation. Fresh start vibes all around, but with a side order of emotional baggage. And you know me, always the bloody knight in slightly dented armour. Those shared vulnerabilities? They built this ridiculously strong, ridiculously fast emotional rollercoaster. My brain, prone to intense fixations, probably zoomed in on her like a heat-seeking missile. New person, deep connection, a project (fixing her!), instant dopamine hit. What could possibly go wrong? (Spoiler alert: everything).

We met up a few weeks later, and bloody hell, the chemistry was like a bloody science experiment gone right. Or wrong, depending on how you look at it. She stayed for a week. A whole week! My house, usually a monument to organised chaos (or just plain chaos), suddenly felt… shared. We were exploring the local countryside, me trying to act like I knew where I was going (spoiler: I rarely do), cooking together (if you include ginger breads in the shape of a penis), talking for hours about everything and nothing. Proper deep emotional intimacy. My brain, usually flitting from one thought to another like a caffeinated butterfly, actually felt… present. Focused. Which, again, was probably the intense novelty of it all. But when she left? Bloody hell. It was like someone had pulled the rug out from under me. This massive wave of anxiety just crashed over me.

Now, here's where it gets properly confusing. Despite this intense, week-long, practically-moved-in situation, she insisted… "just friends." Just. Friends. Right. Like telling a toddler they can have all the sweets they want, as long as they don't eat them. She was still technically married, fair enough, but separated. "Not ready for a relationship," she says. Okay, I can sort of get that. But then comes the kicker: "You can't see anyone else though."

Hang on a minute. So, I'm in this exclusive, non-exclusive, emotionally intimate, platonic-but-not-really… thing. My brain, already wired like a faulty switchboard, was trying to process this logic pretzel and short-circuiting spectacularly.

I became obsessed. Proper Sherlock Holmes-ing her every word, every action, trying to crack the code of her true feelings. My ADHD, bless its cotton socks, went into hyperdrive.

Rejection Sensitive Dysphoria?

Oh, it was having a bloody field day. Every unanswered text, every slightly ambiguous comment, felt like a personal slight, a confirmation that I wasn't good enough. I was constantly on edge, walking on eggshells, terrified of saying or doing the wrong thing, desperate to keep this… whatever it was… going.

The emotional regulation?

Out the window. One minute I was on top of the world when she paid me attention, the next I was spiralling into a pit of despair at the slightest perceived indifference. Fun times.

Even though we had a lot in common – the fitness, the personal growth stuff – she remained emotionally distant, but not so distant. If that makes sense?

Like talking to a particularly attractive brick wall. You could tell she was hurting, lost. And me? Well, with my trusty "Captain Save-Her" cape flapping in the breeze (my therapist loves that nickname), I took it upon myself to fix her. Because that always ends well, doesn't it? It felt like I was the one doing all the heavy lifting in this "situationship." The constant reaching out, the pouring of my heart, the emotional investment that felt about as balanced as a unicycle on a tightrope. My brain, always seeking a purpose, had decided she was my project. Classic BPD, having a favourite person, masked as being a supportive friend.

Our time together? Always on her terms. We'd have these amazing adventures. Hiking through the ridiculously beautiful waterfalls in South Wales, me trying not to slip and plummet to my doom while simultaneously trying to look like a rugged outdoorsman. Discovering these hidden gems in the countryside, places I probably wouldn't have found myself because my internal GPS is powered by hope and guesswork. We made memories that, yeah, I still cherish. But then… poof. She'd disappear back to her life, her family, her responsibilities, leaving me hanging in this limbo of uncertainty and anxiety. My brain would replay those amazing moments over and over, desperately trying to recapture the high, only to crash down again when the reality of her emotional unavailability hit.

And her life? Top secret. Couldn't visit her part of the UK, let alone her actual town. It was like she was living in a bloody spy novel. Communication was sporadic, unpredictable. A text on her way home from work, a quick call on the way to the gym, and then… radio silence for days. I tried to explain the whole ADHD thing, how the inconsistent communication messed with my head, the constant need for reassurance. But it was like talking to a particularly stubborn houseplant. It just wasn't getting it.

Slowly but surely, I was morphing back into a people-pleaser. Saying yes to everything, sacrificing my own needs and boundaries just to keep this fragile connection alive.

And the cocaine?

Yeah, that old "friend" decided to make a reappearance. What started as a "now and then" thing to cope with the emotional rollercoaster became a crutch. Numbing the pain, silencing the doubts, escaping the confusing reality of this bloody situationship. A dangerous spiral, and deep down, I knew it.

The fact that I was popping beta-blockers before doing coke, just to try and stop my heart, was a proper "what the actual hell are you doing?" moment. A terrifying wake-up call that my brain, in its desperate attempt to self-medicate, was leading me down a very dark path.

And the jealousy! Oh, the jealousy. Apparently, having female models in my videos for Attentive was akin to committing some sort of heinous crime. Angry messages, accusations of flirting, of betraying her trust. It was exhausting, demoralising. My brain, already prone to overthinking, would get completely stuck on these accusations, replaying them endlessly, trying to figure out what I'd done wrong. The emotional intensity was just draining.

Then came the morning I finally snapped. I was in Essex, recording a podcast (trying to be all productive and inspirational again), when she just... appeared on my doorstep. Unannounced. Drove three bloody hours to dump a bin bag of stuff she'd accumulated over our year of… whatever it was… on my doorstep. A bin bag of memories. Then, turned around and drove straight back. I came home to this black bin bag of emotional baggage on my doorstep.

The irony?

Whenever I was genuinely down, genuinely sad, or she was down, she couldn't be arsed to drive down the road, let alone three hours. Nor would she let me even send her a bouquet of flowers to try and cheer up, in case her son or brother suspected anything.

Her actions finally screamed louder than her confusing words. And I finally got it. This wasn't healthy. The toxic words we both spewed, mine being even more toxic than the last emotional outburst. This wasn't what either of us deserved. I was more than someone's emotional crutch, someone's secret, someone's convenient distraction. It was time to bloody walk away. Reclaim my power. And focus on putting myself back together, one slightly chaotic, ADHD-riddled piece at a time.

I knew my worth, but healing completely can't be done as a single person.

THE COCAINE CURSE.

Cocaine had become my insidious companion, a toxic elixir that promised escape but delivered only fleeting relief and lasting damage. I used it as a form of self-medication, a desperate attempt to numb the emotional pain and anxiety that plagued me. It wasn't about partying or socialising; in fact, if I ever found myself using it in a social setting, I'd instantly crave the solitude of my own home. The noise, the lights, the social interactions – it all became overwhelming, a sensory overload that only amplified the unease within me.

I'd retreat into my own world, the smallest room in the house – usually my office. I'd draw the curtains throughout the house, close the blinds in whatever room I was in, latch the door, and create a fortress of silence. My phone was always face down. I'd ignore calls and texts. I craved total isolation, where I could fully succumb to the drug's grip. I couldn't drink alcohol without it. Alcohol, a depressant, would amplify the drug's euphoric effects, creating a volatile cocktail of intoxication and oblivion. But as my tolerance grew, so did my dependency. I began using cocaine even when I wasn't drinking. It became my escape. My go-to. My survival tactic. A misguided tool to silence the noise in my head and distance myself from the world.

The paranoia was relentless. It wasn't a side effect – it became my reality. Every creak in the floorboards, every car passing by every gust of wind outside triggered an avalanche of anxiety. I'd glue my eyes to the security cameras on my phone, convinced the police were coming to raid the house, convinced the neighbours could hear everything. I'd hallucinate torches through the frosted front door glass, figures lurking in the shadows. I became a prisoner of my own mind, locked in a self-imposed cell of fear and shame. Hours would pass while I sat in silence, barely breathing, my heart pounding like a drum.

To maintain this facade, I became an expert liar. I deceived the people closest to me. I'd make excuses, cancel plans, claim I was too tired or unwell. I'd fake errands just to disappear for hours. And nobody knew the real reason why. I hated myself for it. The guilt would hit me the moment the high wore off, crashing down like a tidal wave. I'd cry in the mirror. I'd stare at my reflection and ask, "What are you doing? Who even are you anymore?"

The financial toll was enormous. Thousands of pounds – maybe even a house deposit's worth – down the drain. One month, I'd done a shutdown at work and got paid a significant amount. I had enough for a deposit on a house. I went off sick with stress and sniffed the entire amount. In a matter of weeks, it was gone.

It's sickening to think about. Not just the waste, but the fact I would have kept doing it. No savings. No real plan. Just living week to week, chasing a fleeting high that never lasted. The dopamine hit would last minutes. The come down. Hours. Days. It affected my relationships, my business, my creativity. I was less motivated, less present, less myself.

The hole in my septum is now a physical reminder of what I did to myself. My nose bleeds easily. Sometimes, even blowing it is painful. Towards the end of my addiction, I would cry while using it. Every time. Tears would fall down my cheeks because I knew I was damaging myself, I knew I was risking everything, but I couldn't stop. I'd convince myself I had a collapsed septum, check the mirror obsessively, panic that I was permanently disfigured. And then I'd do another line. That's how warped the thinking becomes.

The turning point was slow, but it started with those tears. With the fear. With the realisation that I was living a double life. That even when good things happened – even when my brand was growing, when I found meaning in helping others – I was still being dragged under by this substance.

I have never touched cocaine since meeting Nik. And I never will.

But I have come close! Closer than I like to admit. I still get urges. Still feel that little voice whisper when I'm in a pub or walk past somewhere I used to sniff lines in the toilet. It's like my subconscious keeps score – remembers where, when and who. Like there's a part of my brain still mapping out sessions, just in case.

That's why I had to let go of people I used to call friends. Not because I hated them – but because being around them would make my skin itch with temptation. The old me itched to come back. All it would take was a look, a nod, a bag. I couldn't risk it. I had to choose myself. I had to choose my family.

With my exes, I used to fake migraines. I'd ignore their calls while telling myself I was just tired - all while sat alone, high, locked away, heart racing, volume barely on 1%, trying to convince myself I was still in control.

Nik has never had that version of me. Not because of luck – but because I changed. I chose to change.

The cocaine curse didn't end the night I stopped sniffing. It ended the day I stopped running from myself. The day I started telling the truth.

And the truth is… I still fight it. But now I fight for something bigger. I fight for her. I fight for us. I fight for me.

Getting sober wasn't as simple as making a promise, though. It took therapy. Self-discipline. Routine. Accountability. It took medication. Structure. Community. It took me learning about my ADHD and the reason I was using cocaine in the first place. I wasn't trying to party. I was trying to medicate.

I needed stimulation. Cocaine was the wrong solution, but it was effective – until it wasn't.

I had to change everything. My environment. My habits. My emotional responses. I started leaning into the things that supported my mind: high-protein meals, cold water therapy, fitness, routine, spirituality. Boxing became a huge part of my recovery. I channelled my energy into the ring instead of the mirror. I faced fear head-on, but in a constructive way. Every punch, every round, was a step away from the past and toward something better.

The emotional toll of recovery is intense. It doesn't end with putting the drug down. That's when the real work starts. You must feel everything you've been avoiding. You must sit with the shame, the regret, the pain. I had to forgive myself. I had to apologise to the people I hurt, even if they never knew the full extent of what I was doing. I had to look in the mirror and say, "You were doing the best you could with the tools you had at the time. Now it's time to get better tools."

The first few weeks sober was hell. My hands trembled, my skin felt like it didn't fit right and my mind was screaming for something – anything – to numb the noise. I couldn't sleep. I sweated through my sheets every night. I avoided my mates. Not because I was strong - but because I didn't trust myself. I thought recovery would be peaceful. It felt like war. But for the first time, I was a war I actually wanted to win.

Long-term healing isn't glamorous. It's mundane. It's waking up early and drinking water. It's skipping the night out. It's eating properly, moving your body, managing your medication, going to therapy. It's deleting numbers from your phone. Blocking dealers. Avoiding triggers. It's talking about your cravings when they come – and they do come. But the cravings pass. And over time, they get weaker.

Now, I don't recognise the person I used to be. And I'm so glad. I'm proud of the man I am today. A man who is present. Honest. Clear-headed. Creative. Focused. A father. A partner. A friend. An advocate. A survivor.

Cocaine nearly ruined me. But it didn't win. I'm still here. Stronger. Wiser. Sober. And I wouldn't trade that for anything.

To anyone battling addiction: you're not weak. You're not broken. You're not alone. Healing is possible. Recovery is real. And life, on the other side of that high, is more beautiful than you can imagine.

THE THERAPY ODYSSEY.

My journey through therapy has been anything but linear. It's been a slow burn over years, with moments of clarity followed by long stretches of confusion. I started therapy when I was seventeen. Back then, I didn't have the vocabulary for what I was feeling I just knew something wasn't right. My mind felt like a runaway train, and I couldn't find the brakes. Therapy seemed like the only option. But with each attempt, I was trying to fix something I didn't understand yet. I was trying to fix me—but without knowing why I was the way I was; it was like treating symptoms without ever finding the root cause.

Before I was diagnosed with ADHD, therapy felt like navigating in the dark. Every new therapist, every different approach, offered a glimmer of hope—a small torch in the fog. I tried one-on-one CBT first. It gave me some techniques, some logic to help calm the chaos. I learned how to challenge negative thoughts, how to reframe my thinking. But it felt clinical. Surface-level. Like trying to plug holes in a dam that was seconds from bursting.

Then came group CBT. It was comforting in some ways—being surrounded by others who were clearly struggling too reminded me that I wasn't completely alone. But the sessions often focused on trauma, and those sessions felt more like emotional minefields than safe spaces. I'd leave more exhausted than when I arrived, dredging up childhood pain without having the tools to process it properly.

Anger management was another detour. People around me always said I needed to get a grip on my temper. I believed them. I didn't realise at the time that my anger wasn't just a behavioural issue—it was coming from the emotional dysregulation that comes with ADHD. It wasn't rage for the sake of it; it was frustration from not being able to process things properly, from being constantly misunderstood, from the pressure bubbling just under the surface. That's the part no one ever talks about—the shame that follows the outbursts, the regret, the deep self-loathing.

I sought out therapy mainly in moments of crisis. After breakups. After making impulsive decisions I regretted. After scaring myself with my own behaviour. I'd always go back in with the same mission: to figure out how to be the partner someone could love. Therapy wasn't about me back then—it was about saving whatever relationship I'd just wrecked. And because my ADHD was still undiagnosed, no therapist could fully piece it together either. We were always working on the wrong puzzle.

I started to believe the problem was purely chemical. Maybe my hormones were out of whack. I went to my GP more times than I can count, convinced my testosterone was the issue. I wanted a scientific answer. Something I could fix with a pill. Instead, I got antidepressants. Repeatedly. Different names, different doses. They didn't help. I didn't feel numb, or better—I just felt nothing. Or worse. More detached. Flatter. My problem wasn't a lack of serotonin—it was a brain that was constantly starving for dopamine.

Then came the diagnosis. ADHD. And suddenly, it all started to make sense.

The late diagnosis was like a plot twist I should have seen coming. My whole life up until that point had been shaped by a brain that worked differently—and I'd had no idea. My impulsivity, my inability to focus, my emotional rollercoasters—it wasn't just poor self-control. It was neurological. That diagnosis was equal parts relief and grief. Relief that I finally had an answer. Grief for the years I spent believing I was broken.

Post-diagnosis, I dove into schema therapy. It helped me trace patterns—how unmet emotional needs as a child had shaped my adult behaviours. How I'd built entire defence mechanisms around being abandoned or dismissed. ADHD life coaching followed, and that changed everything. For the first time, I had someone helping me build strategies tailored to my brain, not just telling me to try harder or think differently. My coach helped me find structure. Systems. Accountability. Without her support, I honestly don't know if I'd still be here. I used to joke I wouldn't make it past 30. It wasn't really a joke.

Medication was a whole different battle. The first ADHD med I was given didn't go well. It made me feel hypersexual, almost obsessive—it triggered a version of me I didn't recognise, and not in a good way. When I was switched to Elvanse, things got better. Slowly. I titrated up carefully, keeping notes on everything—focus, mood, appetite. 70mg was the sweet spot at first. I felt clearer, more in control. Like I was finally driving the car instead of just being dragged behind it. But as I gained more self-awareness, I realised I didn't need to be maxed out. I reduced the dose to 50mg, and the balance felt right.

At one point, I was also diagnosed with borderline personality disorder. A label that explained the emotional volatility and intense reactions I'd always had. Another missing puzzle piece. The BPD diagnosis gave context to the extreme highs and lows, the way I could go from infatuation to fear of abandonment in seconds. To help stabilise those swings, I was prescribed Venlafaxine. The combination of Elvanse and Venlafaxine gave me a version of myself I could manage. It didn't fix everything—but it gave me space to breathe.

Over time, I learned that trauma doesn't have to be dramatic to be damaging. You don't need to be physically abused to have trauma. Sometimes, not having your emotional needs met as a child can be just as impactful. Sometimes, not knowing why you feel different is enough to leave lasting scars. My biggest trauma, I've come to realise, was not being diagnosed with ADHD until adulthood. Living a life built around the wrong framework. Being punished for things I couldn't control. That's what shaped me.

Therapy isn't a one-size-fits-all. It's taken me years to find what works, to understand what I need and when. It's a mixture of reflection, strategy, medication, support, and self-compassion. Most importantly, it's a commitment to never stop trying. To keep learning, keep growing. Not for someone else. Not to save a relationship. But for me.

This therapy journey—my therapy odyssey—hasn't been easy. But it's been worth it. It's helped me uncover who I really am beneath the mess. Not someone broken. Just someone who needed to be understood. And finally, I feel like I am.

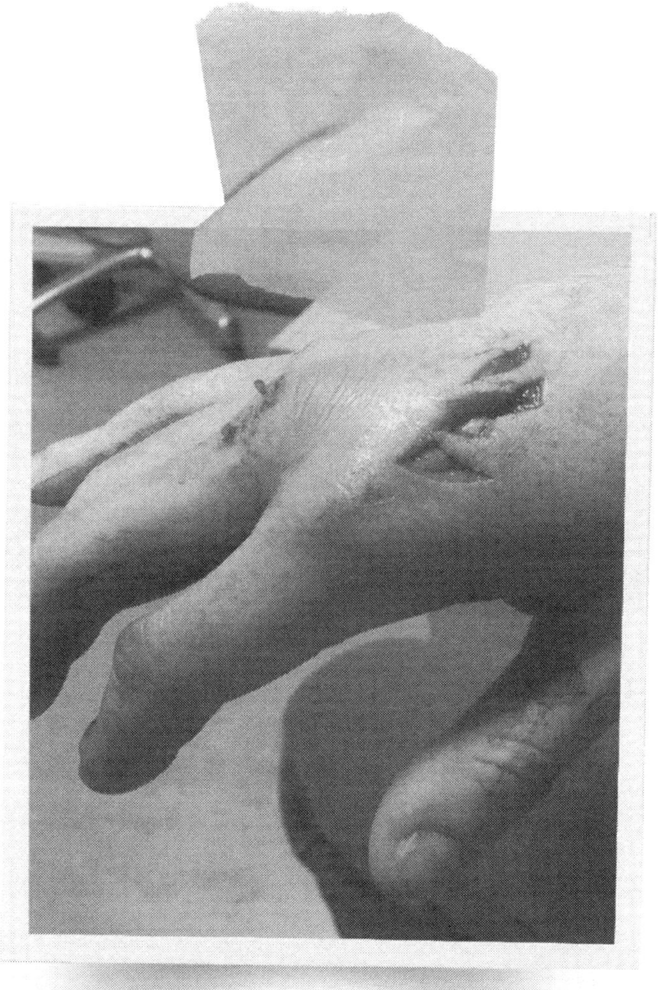

THE JEKYLL AND HYDE WITHIN.

The diagnosis of borderline personality disorder (BPD) was a watershed moment, a turning point that offered both clarity and complexity. It is something I had explored for years, but never fully knew how to explain to people. It explained the emotional intensity, the impulsivity, and the turbulent relationships that had characterized my life. My anger was more than anger; it was an uncontrollable rage; one I knew was more than an ADHD meltdown. It was as if a veil had been lifted, revealing the hidden patterns and underlying causes of my struggles.

For years, I had grappled with a sense of inner turmoil, a feeling that something was fundamentally different about the way I experienced and processed emotions. The world seemed to operate on a different emotional frequency, and I was constantly struggling to tune in, to understand the nuances of social interaction, to regulate the tidal waves of feeling that threatened to overwhelm me.

The BPD diagnosis, coupled with my earlier ADHD diagnosis, was like finally finding the missing pieces of the puzzle, the keys to understanding the intricate workings of my brain. It was a profound realization, a validation of my experiences, and a catalyst for self-acceptance. Suddenly, the chaotic symphony of my inner world began to make sense. The impulsivity, the emotional reactivity, the intense fear of abandonment, the black-and-white thinking – it all had a name, a framework for understanding, a path toward healing.

With the diagnosis came the prescription of Venlafaxine, an SNRI antidepressant. This medication, while not a cure-all, has been a valuable tool in managing my symptoms. It has helped to regulate my mood, reducing the intensity of my emotional swings, smoothing out the sharp peaks and valleys that had once defined my emotional landscape. The once-overwhelming emotions, the all-consuming anger and despair, the crippling anxiety that would grip me without warning – they have become more manageable, allowing me to respond to situations with greater thoughtfulness and empathy.

It's not that I no longer feel deeply; it's that I now have the tools to navigate those emotions with greater awareness and control. The medication, combined with schema therapy and self-awareness, has provided a sense of stability, a foundation upon which I can build a more fulfilling and balanced life.

Before my diagnosis and subsequent treatment, I experienced episodes of what I now understand to be splitting. It was as if a switch flipped, transforming me into a different person, a stranger inhabiting my own body. My pupils would dilate, my heart would race, and I would enter a state of heightened emotional arousal, a fight-or-flight response triggered by perceived threats or perceived abandonment.

It was like a volcano erupting, the molten lava of my emotions overflowing, scorching everything in its path. I would say and do things that I would later deeply regret, things that would hurt the people I loved most, words that would cut like knives, actions that would leave lasting scars. It was like a Jekyll and Hyde transformation, the charming, empathetic person I believed myself to be giving way to a dark, destructive alter ego.

During these episodes, I would black out, losing touch with reality, my actions dictated by a primal rage and an overwhelming sense of fear. It was like a blackout curtain falling over my consciousness, leaving me a prisoner to my impulses. I would say the worst possible things, knowing full well how they would hurt the other person, yet feeling powerless to stop myself. The words would tumble out of my mouth, venomous and cruel, laced with a bitterness that

I didn't even recognize as my own. It was as if I was possessed by a malevolent force, a dark side that took control of my thoughts and actions, leaving me a mere spectator in my own body, watching in horror as the destruction unfolded. The aftermath of these episodes was always fraught with guilt and shame.

I would start to think logically, the fog of the episode lifting, filled with remorse and regret. I would apologize profusely, but the damage was done. The trust had been broken, the relationships strained, and the self-loathing would consume me.

My now understanding of the condition, along with therapy and medication, has helped me understand and manage these episodes. I am now more aware of the triggers that can lead to these dissociative states – perceived rejection, abandonment, or criticism.

I've learned to recognize the subtle cues, the shift in tone, the flicker of disapproval in someone's eyes, the seemingly innocuous comment that triggers a cascade of insecurity and fear. I am able to recognize the early warning signs – the racing heart, the feeling of being attacked, the tightening in my chest – and take steps to prevent them from escalating.

I've learned to remove myself from triggering situations, to practice grounding techniques, to reach out for support, to breathe deeply and remind myself that I am safe, that I am loved, that I am not my emotions. And when they do occur, I am better equipped to manage the aftermath, to apologize sincerely and to make amends.

But the splitting wasn't just about verbal attacks. It often manifested in self-destructive behaviours, a desperate attempt to regain control, to punish myself for the perceived wrongdoings, to escape the overwhelming emotions and pain I was feeling at the time. I would drive recklessly, pushing my car to its limits, the speedometer hitting over 150 mph at times, as I raced towards a self-imposed oblivion.

When I'd finally snap out of it, the guilt and self-hatred would be unbearable. I'd punch mirrors, unable to stand the sight of the person I had become, the monster that lurked within. It was like an out-of-body experience, watching myself cause so much destruction, powerless to stop the carnage.

The only way I could calm down, to regain a semblance of control, was to inflict physical pain on myself. I'd punch myself in the face, the impact a jarring reminder of my physical presence, a way to ground myself in reality. I'd punch mirrors or smash glass and cut myself, the sharp sting of the cuts a perverse form of release, the sight of my own blood a visceral shock that would snap me out of the dissociative state.

These self-harming episodes often landed me in the hospital, stitches patching up the physical wounds, while the emotional scars lingered, a constant reminder of the battle raging within.

Understanding that BPD is a trauma disorder was a crucial step in my healing journey. It allowed me to connect the dots between my early experiences and my current struggles, to recognize the impact of my undiagnosed ADHD and the unmet emotional needs that had shaped my development. Growing up with ADHD, without the proper support and understanding, created a sense of chronic invalidation, a feeling of being different, misunderstood, and often rejected. This early trauma, coupled with other adverse experiences, contributed to the development of BPD, a complex disorder characterized by intense emotions, black-and-white thinking, and a fragile sense of self.

The journey of recovery is ongoing and will always be a continuous process of self-discovery and healing. But I am grateful for the progress I have made, for the newfound understanding of my own mind, for the tools and strategies that have helped me to manage my symptoms and navigate the challenges of BPD and ADHD. I am learning to accept my imperfections, to forgive myself for past mistakes, and to embrace the person I am becoming.

With each passing day, I am growing stronger, more resilient, and more authentic. The Jekyll and Hyde within is slowly being tamed, the darkness replaced by a growing sense of self awareness, compassion, and hope. I am no longer defined by my diagnoses; I am defined by my strength, my resilience, and my unwavering commitment to healing and growth.

FINDING MY FOREVER.

November 2nd, a date forever etched in my memory, a turning point in the narrative of my life. It was the day I met Nikki, my now fiancé, the woman who would redefine love, rewrite the script of my life, and show me the true meaning of connection. I was exhibiting Attentive Apparel at a local event, my heart brimming with the passion of spreading awareness on neurodiversity, surrounded by the buzz of curious people with neurodivergent conditions. Then, she walked in, a ray of sunshine piercing through the ordinary.

Nikki wasn't my usual type, with her radiant blonde hair and captivating smile, she stood out from the crowd like a beacon of light, in her bright pink 1/4 zip top, leggings and hoodie, an outfit I will remember for eternity. I had always been drawn to brunettes, but something about her presence, her aura, pulled me in like a moth to a flame. She approached my stall, her eyes sparkling with genuine interest, expressing curiosity about the brand and its message. Or so I thought. Little did I know, her interest extended far beyond the clothing; it was me she was drawn to, a connection she felt on a deeper level, she was on her way out, noticed me and something drew her towards me.

When she spoke to me, I was completely flustered. My words caught in my throat, my usual found confidence evaporated, and I stuttered like a schoolboy with a crush. My cheeks flushed crimson, my palms grew sweaty, and I felt a wave of self-consciousness wash over me. I must have made a complete fool of myself, but somehow, through the nervous stammering and awkward pauses, I managed to sell her two hoodies – one for her and one for her son, Olly.

As she walked away, I felt a pang of disappointment, a sense of missed opportunity. I had to get her number, to explore this spark that had ignited within me. I rushed outside for a cigarette, hoping to catch her before she disappeared into the distance, my heart pounding with anticipation and a touch of apprehension. But she was nowhere to be found. Disheartened, I returned to my stall, wondering if I had let a golden opportunity slip through my fingers.

Later that afternoon, as I was grabbing some food after the event, my phone pinged with a notification. An Instagram message from Nikki! My heart skipped a beat, a surge of excitement coursing through my veins. We chatted online for a few days, the conversation flowing effortlessly, like two old friends reuniting after a long separation. We delved into deep conversations about life, love, and the pursuit of happiness, discovering a shared passion for personal growth and a profound connection that transcended the digital realm. It was like I had known her forever, and even though I wasn't looking for anything or anyone, we had soon, planned our first date, eager to explore this undeniable spark in person.

Thursday evening arrived, the same day I had received a barrage of abuse from the woman I had been entangled with, a situationship that had been draining my energy and dimming my light. It was the push I needed to finally cut ties with that negativity and pursue whatever this was with Nikki, a breath of fresh air that promised a new beginning.

We went bowling, and the rest, as they say, is history. The evening was filled with laughter, playful competition, and a sense of ease I had never experienced before. We played arcade games, our competitive spirits igniting with each playful challenge. We tested our skills on the pool table; the green felt a battleground for our playful banter and flirtatious glances. And I even won a kiss from her after a triumphant game of pool, a wager that sealed our fate. That first kiss was magical.

It was gentle, tender, and filled with a sense of familiarity, as if we had known each other forever. It was a kiss that spoke of a deep connection, a recognition of two souls destined to meet. Leaving the bowling alley that night, I felt a lightness in my step, a sense of hope and excitement that I hadn't felt in years. I couldn't wait to see her again, to explore the depths of this newfound connection.

When I got home, I couldn't sleep until I knew she was home safe. This was new, this feeling of genuine care and concern for someone I had just met. There was no anxiety, no overwhelming intensity, just a calm sense of connection that felt incredibly right. It was a refreshing change from the tumultuous relationships of my past, a welcome respite from the drama and chaos that had often accompanied love.

Nikki was different from anyone I had ever met. She was beautiful, intelligent, and had an innate understanding of me and my neurodiversity. I felt safe with her, seen and accepted for who I truly was, quirks and all. There was no need to pretend, no need to mask my ADHD or suppress my emotions. I could be myself, completely and authentically, and she loved me even more for it.

Our connection was like a slow-burning fire, a gradual build-up of warmth and intimacy that felt sustainable and real. It wasn't the instant, intense, overwhelming love I had experienced in the past, the kind that often led to chaos and heartbreak. This was different. This was a love that nurtured and supported, a love that allowed me to grow and thrive, a love that felt like coming home.

All the work I had done on myself, the therapy, being sober, self-reflection, the spiritual awakening – it had all led me to this moment, to this woman who embodied everything I had ever longed for in a partner. And Nikki, with her own journey of self-discovery and healing, was ready to meet me where I was, to embrace my imperfections and celebrate my strengths. The universe had orchestrated our meeting, a cosmic dance of two souls destined to find each other.

I met her children, Olly and Gracie, and my heart grew even fonder. Gracie, with her autistic brilliance and infectious laughter, brought a unique and beautiful energy into my life. Her quirky personality and unwavering love filled my days with joy and wonder. Olly, like me, had ADHD, and we instantly bonded, becoming best friends and partners in crime. We shared a mischievous glint in our eyes, a boundless energy that fuelled our adventures and laughter.

When Nikki's living situation became untenable, they moved into my house. Her flat was a disaster, unsafe and unsuitable for two young children. Gracie, especially, needed stability and routine, and we worried about how she would adapt to such a drastic change. But our fears were unfounded. She settled in immediately, as if she had always belonged there. It felt like destiny, like all the pieces of the puzzle were finally falling into place.

Living with me was a refuge for Nikki, a sanctuary from toxic influences. The stress and anxiety that had plagued her for years began to melt away. She was finally free to be herself, to heal, and to thrive. I watched her blossom, her laughter becoming more frequent, her smile more radiant. It was a privilege to witness her transformation, to be a part of her healing journey.

I knew I wanted them in my life forever. On the 28th of June, at an Airbnb I had rented for the four of us to go away too, something that sort of resembled the telly tubbies house, one of Gracie's favourite programs at the time. After asking Olly for his approval, I asked Nikki to marry me. It was a momentous decision, a testament to the depth of my love and commitment. I had never trusted anyone enough to take that leap before, but with Nikki, it felt natural, inevitable. She was my soulmate, my best friend, the missing piece of my puzzle.

Our love story is a testament to the power of self-work, the magic of the universe, and the undeniable force of destiny. We are two souls who have found each other after years of searching, two flames that have finally reunited. Our connection is more than just coincidence; it's a deep-rooted bond that transcends time and space. We were always meant to be, and I am eternally grateful for the day our paths finally crossed. Our love story is a symphony of serendipity, a testament to the enduring power of hope, healing, and the unwavering belief in true love.

Our journey together, while undeniably magical, hasn't been without its bumps in the road. We are two individuals with strong personalities and certain triggers, and inevitably, there are times when those things are triggered, ending up in an argument.

We've had our fair share of disagreements, moments of frustration, and days where we simply get on each other's nerves. But these moments, these challenges, have only served to strengthen our bond.

We've learned to navigate each other's sensitivities, to recognize the potential triggers that can ignite emotional outbursts. I've come to understand the power of my words, the impact my ADHD-fuelled impulsivity can have on Nikki's sensitive soul and how she reacts to certain situations, due to trauma in her past. She, in turn, has learned to approach my now extremely occasional meltdowns with patience and understanding, offering support and reassurance instead of criticism and judgment.

We've both come to realize that nobody is perfect, that we all make mistakes, say things we regret, and act in ways that can hurt those we love. It's about recognizing those imperfections, forgiving ourselves and each other, and striving to communicate with kindness and compassion. I've learned to challenge my own perceptions, to recognize that my ADHD can sometimes distort my interpretation of reality. It's about giving myself a break, acknowledging that I'm not always going to get it right, and that's okay. Also, recognition of things that can cause a meltdown, such as being tired or forgetting to take my medication has helped to avoid these situations too.

One of the most surprising and beautiful aspects of our relationship is the comfort we find in the ordinary, which in the past is what I would have called being bored. We can spend entire days doing absolutely nothing, simply enjoying each other's company, basking in the quiet contentment of our shared space. There's no pressure to fill every moment with excitement or adventure; we find joy in the simplicity of being together, whether it's cuddling on the sofa, watching a movie, or me doing paperwork but next to her, with our feet touching, but in companionable silence.

We've also learned the importance of open and honest communication. We talk about everything, from the mundane details of our day to the deepest fears and insecurities that lurk beneath the surface. We don't shy away from difficult conversations; we embrace them as opportunities to deepen our understanding and strengthen our connection. We talk through problems before they fester and grow, addressing concerns and insecurities before they have a chance to erode our trust.

And even when triggers inevitably arise, and emotions run high, we make a conscious effort to talk through the experience afterwards. We dissect the trigger, analyse the reaction, and explore ways to navigate similar situations in the future. It's a continuous process of learning and growth, a commitment to understanding each other on a deeper level and creating a safe space for vulnerability and emotional honesty.

Our love story is a testament to the power of communication, compromise, and unwavering support. It's a reminder that even amidst the challenges and imperfections of life, true love can flourish when two souls are committed to growing together, embracing each other's flaws, and celebrating the unique beauty of their shared journey.

Getting in a relationship with Nikki, meant we both had to do work on ourselves, we couldn't do when we were single. But as she understands how my brain works, and that sometimes I can feel rejected by the most trivial of things, and when I am like that, the logical thinking side of my brain basically switches off, until it's passed, and I can think logically again.

THE GIFT OF FAMILY.

Meeting Nikki shifted the entire trajectory of my life, but it was her two incredible children—Gracie and Olly—who gave my heart a purpose I never imagined possible. Before them, I'd never truly considered what it meant to be a father. I thought I had a rough idea from watching others, maybe even from stepping in as "Uncle Chris" to Ryan's kids, who I've always loved like my own. But nothing could have prepared me for the overwhelming, transformative impact these two children would have on me.

From the moment they walked through my door, I knew something had changed. Not just in the atmosphere of my home, but in me. It was subtle at first. The quiet noise of cartoons humming from the TV, the echo of small feet running across the laminate floor, the trail of toys leading from the living room to the kitchen. But within days, that soft change became seismic.

Gracie, with her sparkling eyes and pure, unfiltered emotion, came into my life like a burst of colour I didn't know I was missing. She's beautifully autistic—bright, honest, full of laughter, and deeply intuitive. She doesn't hold back, doesn't mask, doesn't bend to fit the world around her. She is, unapologetically. That kind of honesty was disarming at first. I was used to people hiding things, editing themselves. But Gracie? She speaks her mind with a fierce kind of truth, and it taught me to stop walking on eggshells. To listen without needing to fix. To just be present.

She taught me patience, not the shallow kind where you wait for someone to hurry up, but the real, soul-deep kind. The kind where you learn to sit in the chaos of a meltdown and just breathe. To find a way through together. Watching her navigate the world, with her own rhythms and needs, challenged everything I thought I knew about connection and communication. And the way she trusts me now—the way she throws her arms around me after a long day or tucks herself beside me under a blanket to watch her favourite shows—those are moments I hold tight.

Then there's Olly—my little twin flame. Diagnosed with ADHD like me, it's like looking into a younger version of myself, only without the years of shame and confusion I carried before I knew what it was. We clicked instantly. We play football until it's dark, shoot hoops until we can't feel our arms, and laugh over the silliest things for hours. He's my teammate, my gaming partner, my sidekick in mischief. But he's more than just fun—he's perceptive. He notices when I'm low. He asks questions that catch me off guard. "Are you OK today, Chris?" he'll ask, looking up at me with that serious little face. And it knocks the wind out of me every time.

I remember one night sitting outside on the garden step after a tough week. I was overwhelmed—work stress, bills, trying to be the man I wanted to be for all of them. Olly came out, sat next to me silently for a few minutes, then leaned in and said, "I think we're doing OK, you know. It's good having you here." I could've cried on the spot. That moment will stay with me forever.

Before I knew it, they weren't just "Nikki's kids." They were our kids. My world started revolving around school runs, meal planning, reward charts, and bedtime routines. My house, once quiet and minimalistic, became a living, breathing home. There's glitter in the carpet. Lego under the couch. Football boots by the front door. And I wouldn't have it any other way.

Being part of their lives hasn't just changed my routine—it's changed me. It softened me, grounded me, made me care about things I never used to think twice about. I find myself googling how to build sensory-friendly spaces, reading articles about ADHD in kids, researching the best night lights for neurodivergent sleepers. I care about the details because they matter to them.

I've learned to pause before I react. To ask instead of assuming. To explain instead of scold. It's not perfect—I still get overwhelmed, still raise my voice sometimes, still forget that not everything needs to be "fixed." But I'm learning, and they give me grace every step of the way.

My relationship with Nikki grew deeper because of them too. We became a team in the truest sense—co-regulating when things got tense, tag-teaming bedtime routines, having those "we'll laugh about this later" kind of days where everything goes wrong but we pull each other through. Watching her be a mum is one of the most beautiful things I've ever witnessed. She's strong and soft in equal measure, fierce when she needs to be and gentle when it matters most. Seeing her with them makes me love her more every day.

We've had moments where we had to navigate hard stuff together—meltdowns, school transitions, sensory overloads, emotional dysregulation. There have been tears, tantrums (theirs and mine), and times where I questioned whether I was cut out for this. But then a drawing from Grace appears on my desk that says, "Chris, I love you," or Olly shouts from the living room, "Come play FIFA!" and I'm reminded that love isn't about having all the answers. It's about showing up.

I'm proud of who I've become since they entered my life. I'm more empathetic, more aware, more intentional. I've stopped needing everything to be tidy or make sense. I've started embracing the mess, the noise, the chaos of family life—because that's where the joy is. In the middle of the madness, in the cuddles during a movie, in the laughter that fills the room when we're all piled onto the sofa eating popcorn.

And more than anything, I'm grateful. Grateful for Nikki trusting me enough to bring me into her children's lives. Grateful for the bond we've built. Grateful for the unconditional love those kids give me every day. Because the truth is, I thought I knew love. I thought I understood what it meant to care for someone. But being "dad" to these two? It's a whole new world. One I never knew I needed, but now, can't imagine living without.

Gracie and Olly aren't just part of my life—they are my life. They've given me purpose, shaped my identity, and helped me grow in ways I never thought possible. They didn't just change the picture—they transformed the whole canvas. And for that, I will be forever in their debt.

BECOMING AUTHENTICALLY ME.

The journey of self-discovery is a winding path, filled with unexpected twists and turns, moments of profound insight, and periods of frustrating setbacks. Looking back, I can see how far I've come, how much I've changed. But the truth is, I haven't changed so much as I've just become authentically me. I've shed the masks I wore, the roles I played, the expectations I tried to fulfil. I've stripped away the layers of conditioning and society's pressure, revealing the true essence of who I am, a person I am finally proud to be.

It's been a process of shedding and embracing, of letting go of what no longer serves me and welcoming the parts of myself I had long suppressed. The journey has been guided by a series of transformative experiences, each one a catalyst for growth and self-awareness.

Before, I was a ship lost at sea, tossed about by the waves of emotion and impulse, with no compass to guide me. I was reactive, easily triggered, and often overwhelmed by the intensity of my own feelings. My undiagnosed ADHD fuelled a constant state of internal chaos, a whirlwind of thoughts and emotions that I struggled to control. I was a prisoner of my own mind, trapped in a cycle of self-sabotage and impulsive decisions.

Now, I stand at the helm of my own ship, charting my course with intention and purpose. I am no longer at the mercy of my impulses; I have the tools and self-awareness to navigate the challenges that life throws my way. I am calmer, more grounded, and more in control of my emotions. I am the captain of my own destiny, steering my ship towards a horizon of self-acceptance and fulfilment.

The journey has been long and arduous, but the transformation has been profound. Let me share the key experiences that have shaped this evolution:

Boxing:

With its raw physicality and demand for mental discipline, boxing taught me the power of channelling my energy and emotions. It helped me to confront my aggression, to understand my limits, and to discover a strength I never knew I possessed. It was a physical manifestation of the inner battle I was fighting, a way to confront my demons and emerge victorious. Where I once lashed out in anger, I now channel that energy into disciplined movement and focused action. Knowing that lashing out can mean getting punched back, and being punched in the face has a funny way of humbling you.

Schema Therapy:

This deep dive into my past unearthed the roots of my insecurities and self-sabotaging behaviours. It illuminated the impact of early childhood experiences on my adult life, helping me to understand the origins of my emotional patterns and relationship dynamics. Healing my inner child, making little Chris feel safe and when I did that, things didn't trigger me so badly. Schema therapy provided a roadmap for healing, a way to rewrite the outdated scripts that were holding me back. Where I once reacted from a place of deep-seated insecurity, I now respond with self-awareness and compassion. If little Chris is happy, older Chris is happy!

Getting an ADHD Diagnosis:

A lot of people are extremely ignorant as to why people need a diagnosis. I always respond with, "If you had cancer, would you want to know?" My diagnosis was a revelation, a key that unlocked the mysteries of my own mind. It explained the lifelong struggles with focus, impulsivity, and emotional regulation and even made me understand why I was addicted to cocaine. It was my way of self-medicating with stimulants, as it made my mind quiet. My diagnosis gave me permission to be different, to embrace my neurodiversity, and to challenge the societal expectations that had never quite fit. It was a liberation, a validation of my experience, and a catalyst for self-acceptance. Where I once felt like a failure, I now understand that my brain is simply wired differently and I could be gentle and kinder to myself, leading to forgiveness for things I once beat myself up about.

Cutting Out Toxic People:

This was a necessary act of self-preservation, a painful but essential step in creating a life of authenticity and peace. It was a letting go of relationships that had once held meaning and significance but were ultimately hindering my growth and well-being. It was an act of empowerment, a reclaiming of my own worth and a commitment to surrounding myself with people who supported my journey and celebrated my authentic self. Where I once sought validation from others, I now find it within myself. The hardest person you have to let go of is your older self. The person who has basically kept you alive through whatever unhealthy coping mechanisms you have picked up. Letting go of the old you is the hardest goodbye of all.

Learning About My ADHD Brain:

This was like being handed an instruction manual after a lifetime of fumbling in the dark. It allowed me to understand my strengths and weaknesses, to recognize my triggers and develop strategies for managing my symptoms. It was a journey of self-education, a deep dive into the intricacies of my neurology that empowered me to take control of my life and thrive in my own unique way. Where I once felt overwhelmed and confused by my own mind, I now navigate its complexities with greater understanding and self-compassion.

Cold Water Therapy:

Cold water therapy can increase dopamine levels in the blood by up to 250%. With its shock to the system and invigorating embrace, cold water therapy became a ritual of resilience. It was a way to challenge my comfort zone, to face my fears, and to emerge stronger and more invigorated. It was a metaphor for life itself, a reminder that even in the face of discomfort and adversity, I could find the strength to persevere. Where I once shied away from discomfort, I now embrace it as an opportunity for growth. It also helps reduce depressive moods and helps lower cortisol in your body, cortisol being the stress hormone your body produces.

Setting Boundaries:

Establishing clear boundaries, both with myself and others, was a crucial step in reclaiming my power and protecting my well-being. It was about learning to say no, to prioritize my needs, and to honour my own limits. It was about communicating my expectations clearly and respectfully and refusing to tolerate behaviour that violated my sense of self-worth. Where I once allowed others to dictate my boundaries, I now stand firm in my convictions.

Embracing Imperfection:

Realizing that perfection is an impossible task was a liberating revelation. It allowed me to let go of the unrealistic expectations I had set for myself, to embrace my imperfections, and to celebrate my progress rather than constantly striving for an unattainable ideal. It was about accepting myself, flaws, and all, and recognizing that true beauty lies in authenticity. Where I once chased an illusion of perfection, I now embrace the messy, imperfect reality of being human.

Forgiving Myself:

Forgiving myself for the hurt I had caused others in the past was a crucial step in my healing journey. I reached out to ex-partners, offering sincere apologies and acknowledging the pain I had inflicted. It wasn't about seeking absolution or even a reply, it was about taking responsibility for my actions and making amends where possible. It was about letting go of the guilt and shame that had haunted me for years, allowing myself to move forward with a clear conscience and a renewed sense of hope. Where I once carried the weight of past mistakes, I now move forward with forgiveness and self-compassion.

Embracing Sobriety:

Letting go of alcohol and drugs was a crucial turning point in my journey. It was about reclaiming my power from substances that had once controlled me, about choosing clarity and presence over fleeting escapes. It was about honouring my body and mind and creating a life of sustainable well-being. Where I once sought solace in substances, I now find it in healthy habits and mindful practices.

Nourishing My Body and Mind:

Adopting a high-protein diet was more than just a physical choice; it was an act of self-care that supported my mental and emotional well-being. Protein, with its ability to enhance the effectiveness of ADHD medication and promote serotonin production in the gut, became a cornerstone of my nutritional strategy. Prioritizing sleep, ensuring I got adequate rest each night, was another crucial element in managing my ADHD and maintaining a balanced mood.

Embracing ADHD Medication:

For me, ADHD medication has been a game-changer. It has provided the support I needed to manage my symptoms, to focus my energy, and to regulate my emotions. It's not a magic fix, but it has been an invaluable tool in my journey towards self-discovery and fulfilment.

Finding My Tribe:

Surrounding myself with supportive, like-minded people has been essential to my growth and well-being. It's about finding my tribe, the people who understand my struggles, celebrate my strengths, and encourage me to be my authentic self. It's about creating a safe space where I can be vulnerable, share my challenges, and receive unconditional support.

Embracing my authentic self, with all its quirks and imperfections, has been the most liberating experience of all. It's about letting go of the need to please others, to conform to societal expectations, or to pretend to be someone I'm not. It's about celebrating my unique strengths, accepting my limitations, and living a life that is true to my values and passions. It's about being me, fully and unapologetically. It's about recognizing that my journey, with all its ups and downs, has led me to a place of self-acceptance and inner peace. And that is a victory worth celebrating.

LOTTIE BEA.

Before Nikki, I had quietly accepted the idea that I might never have children of my own. Not in a bitter or resentful way, but more in a sense of quiet surrender. I'd spent years in chaotic relationships, failed situationships, and destructive patterns that made me feel like fatherhood was something reserved for more stable, grounded men—men who had it together. I adored Ryan's kids and treated them like family, always ready with presents, cuddles, or a day out. But in the back of my mind, I had already had the tough conversation with my mum—the one where I explained she might not get a grandchild from me. It hurt, more than I let on.

My own history with intimacy didn't help. For as long as I could remember, I'd struggled with climaxing during sex. It wasn't something I shouted from the rooftops, but it was a massive part of my internal shame. My mind was always racing, distracted, unable to fully settle into the moment. The few times it did happen felt like accidents, rare moments of alignment where everything just clicked. But mostly, it didn't. The introduction of Venlafaxine for my BPD only intensified the problem. One of its side effects—delayed ejaculation—was like pouring fuel on a fire that had already been burning for years.

And then came Nikki. She wasn't just the love of my life—she was the calm in the storm I'd been waiting for. With her came Gracie and Olly, two incredible children who filled my world with purpose. Watching myself become a father figure to them stirred something in me I didn't know existed. It ignited a longing. Not just to be a stepdad or a support system, but to have a child that was biologically mine. A little person who shared my DNA, who could carry forward the legacy of healing I'd started. I never said it out loud, but Nikki saw it in me.

Despite having two children already and being on a waiting list for a hysterectomy due to ongoing health issues, Nikki looked me in the eye one day and said, "I don't want to deny you the chance to have your own child."

Her selflessness floored me. She had no reason to offer that gift. But she did. And that moment will forever be etched in my heart as one of the most generous and loving acts I've ever experienced.

Trying for a baby was nothing like I imagined it would be. It wasn't romantic or spontaneous—it was strategic, practical, and emotionally loaded. But it was real. And when Nikki got pregnant for the first time, we were over the moon. That joy was short-lived. The first pregnancy ended in miscarriage. It was devastating, and even though we hadn't been trying for long, it hit like a freight train. The loss cracked something open in both of us, but we held each other close and decided to try again.

The second time, it worked. And suddenly, "Little Bea," our affectionate nickname for the baby, became more than just a hope. It became a heartbeat on a screen, a growing bump, a flutter in Nikki's belly.

Nikki's previous trauma—losing her son George at full term—loomed over us like a dark cloud. Every scan, every twinge, every quiet moment was a trigger. I watched helplessly as she spiralled through fear, panic, and anxiety on a daily basis. I felt it too. Every hospital trip made my stomach turn. Every specialist scan at Tommy's in Manchester filled me with both dread and hope. There wasn't a day that went by that I didn't imagine the worst.

Christmas and New Year weren't about tinsel and fairy lights. They were about antiseptic hospital corridors, emergency appointments, stress, and trying to keep a sense of normality for Gracie and Olly. Watching Gracie, who thrives on routine and safety, try to understand why her mum was always at the hospital broke my heart. I tried to be everything they needed—present, stable, calm—but inside, I was barely holding it together.

My parents stepped in like superheroes. I don't know how we would have survived that season without them. They scooped up the kids, managed logistics, and gave us room to fall apart when we needed it. I cried in bathrooms, in work vans, in the rare quiet moments between hospital runs. I didn't want to put more pressure on Nikki. She was already carrying so much, emotionally, and physically. I learned how to hide it. But it didn't make the fear any less real.

When Nikki started showing signs of early labour—before the scheduled C-section—I knew everything was about to change. The fear peaked. Watching her disappear behind those double doors to the surgery room, knowing I couldn't follow, was unbearable. I wanted to rip the world apart to make sure she was safe.

Then she arrived. Lottie Bea. My daughter.

She didn't come into the world easily. She came covered in wires, her tiny body too fragile to breathe on its own, and my heart broke into a million pieces. I wanted to hold her, to kiss her head, to tell her she was safe—but I wasn't allowed to even touch her. I stood there, watching her chest rise and fall under artificial help, and I felt like I was floating above myself.

The days in special care felt like purgatory. We were stuck in a space between birth and bonding. I was a father, but I didn't feel like one. Nikki was healing, emotionally and physically, and I was splitting myself between her, the kids at home, work, and a baby I couldn't even hold properly. I kept showing up, but inside, I was wrecked. There were moments I questioned if the connection would ever come. Guilt consumed me.

I'd sit in special care, holding Lottie whilst Nikki cried next to me. And all I could feel was the weight of a thousand uncried tears sitting on my chest. Every beep from the machine felt like a bomb going off in m y head. And the worst part? I was sober. Before I'd numb this. Coke, drink, distraction – anything. But now I had to feel it all. Raw. Real. And it fucking hurt. More than I thought I could bare. But I did bare it, well so I thought. But I didn't crack to the urges, and that's how I know I've changed.

When Lottie was born, I didn't cry. I didn't burst with joy. I just felt… nothing. Not because I didn't care – but because I was so fucking overwhelmed I didn't have the words for it. My head was battered. I was sat there trying to figure out why I wasn't feeling how I was "supposed" to feel. The love didn't come rushing like in some Hollywood moment – it crept in slowly, quietly, behind the fear, the guilt and the crushing pressure.

For those few days, I was emotionally numb, yet somehow feeling more than I have ever felt in my entire life. It was like my nervous system was short-circuiting. I wasn't prepared for the weight of it all. I kept thinking, "what the fuck is wrong with me?" But now I know – there was nothing wrong. I was a man who'd been through hell, trying to process the biggest moment of his life with no tools, no emotional training and no fucking clue how to handle it.

When I first held her, it wasn't joy that hit me – it was fear. Fear I'd ruin her. Fear she'd turn out like the worst versions of me in the past. My hands shook so bad I thought I'd drop her. I didn't feel like a man – I felt like a scared little boy holding a mirror. I wanted to protect her from everything, but I had only just started to protect myself.

And then… we got the call. We could bring her home.

I'll never forget the moment I clicked her car seat into place and looked at her sleeping face. Something in me cracked wide open. That connection I'd been waiting for? It hit me like a freight train. I felt it in my bones, in my chest, in every fibre of my being. That was my daughter. My blood. My miracle. From that day forward, everything changed. It hit me so hard, it nearly knocked me off my feet. And in that moment, all I could think was, "don't you dare fuck this up!"

The way I move through the world shifted. My priorities, my perspective, even my pace. I no longer cared about things I used to chase. Cars, money, ego—all of it felt empty compared to the weight of her in my arms, the smell of her head, the sound of her breathing on my chest. Every time I feed her, every time I rock her to sleep, I think about the version of me who never thought this would happen. Who thought he wasn't capable. Who thought he wasn't worthy.

This little girl has given my life a new chapter, a new meaning, a new heart. She's the full stop to a sentence I've been writing my entire life—a story of chaos, of recovery, of love, of healing. And her name? It holds it all. Lottie Bea Maddocks. A name rooted in softness, in warmth, in survival.

I would go through every mistake, every heartbreak, every dark night of the soul all over again just to hold her one more time. She was worth it all.

And as mad as it sounds… if I hadn't started Attentive Apparel, I wouldn't have gone to that local event. I wouldn't have met Nikki. I wouldn't be holding this tiny, perfect girl in my arms. That's the magic of life—the way every chaotic, painful twist can lead you somewhere beautiful if you hold on long enough.

So, if you're reading this, wondering if you'll ever get there… you will. Keep going.

Lottie is proof that even broken men can build beautiful things. That healing is possible. That peace is real. And that sometimes, the best gifts in life come swaddled in a blanket, with tired eyes and a fierce little heartbeat.

I'm her dad. And I'll never take that for granted.

CHAPTER X: THE SILENT STORM

I'd already written this book when this happened.

I thought the story was complete. I thought I'd closed the chapter on everything I wanted to say. But then life—being life—threw something at me that I couldn't ignore. Something that happened after I put the final full stop on the last page.

And I realised… this needed to be added.

Because this chapter shows that no matter how much self-awareness you gain, how much healing you do, or how well you think you understand your brain—mental health isn't linear.

Sometimes, even when everything says you should feel joy, your world quietly falls apart.

This chapter is here to show just that. To be honest about how low things got after I thought I had it all figured out. To show how fragile we all still are, even when we've done the work. And to remind anyone reading that you are not weak just because you're still struggling.

If sharing this helps even one person feel less alone, then writing it—and reliving it—was more than worth it.

The months leading up to Lottie's birth were some of the most terrifying and emotionally suffocating days I've ever lived through.

But I didn't tell anyone that.

Not properly.

On the outside, I played the role—supportive partner, steady stepdad, business owner. The one holding it all together. But inside? I was falling apart in slow motion—too scared to say it, too stubborn to stop it, and too worried about everyone else to ask for help myself.

Nikki's pregnancy wasn't smooth. Because of her medical history, there was always a very real, very heavy possibility that something could go wrong. And then came that conversation—the one I still hear in my head sometimes when the world is quiet.

"If it comes down to me or the baby," Nikki said, "you choose the baby."

How do you even respond to that? I said I understood, but nothing about it felt okay. It was like agreeing to lose the love of my life in advance. From that moment on, I stopped expressing what I was feeling. I shut it all down. Buried it. Told myself to man up. Be strong. Don't make her worry.

I had panic buried under duty. Heartache buried under routine.

And that numbness slowly took over.

To the point where I lost a good friend—and I didn't cry. I didn't even feel it in the way I should have. We'd seen each other just weeks before, laughing and catching up. That turned out to be the last time. But I had so much stress and fear already stuffed into my system, there wasn't space to process his death. I wasn't avoiding grief—I was too full to even let it in.

Nikki was in and out of hospital constantly. And I mean constantly. She didn't want to see anyone except one professor at Glan Clwyd Hospital. I respected that—it was her body, her fear, her decision. But practically, it meant endless 30-minute drives there and back, sometimes multiple times a week.

Meanwhile, I was doing the school runs for Olly and Grace, managing Attentive, trying to respond to customers, keep up with orders, and hold a business together with one hand while keeping a family from unravelling with the other.

I was doing over a thousand miles a week. Easy.

And still, I didn't say a word.

I didn't want to stress Nikki out more than she already was. Grace didn't understand why her mum kept disappearing, and I didn't want her worrying either. So, I kept smiling. Kept saying everything was fine. But inside, I was fraying at the seams.

The week before Lottie arrived, Nikki made the call to stay in hospital until the birth. She was emotionally and physically exhausted. That week crawled by. I hardly slept. I was running on autopilot—drop the kids off, go to the hospital, check in on Nikki, sort dinner, reply to customers, drive back, get a few hours' rest, repeat.

And then… the day came.

24th January 2025. One week before her planned C-section. Four weeks before full term. Lottie was born.

It should have been one of the happiest days of my life.

But I didn't feel happy. I didn't feel anything. Just tension, confusion, and guilt.

I remember watching the medical team take her away almost immediately. A tiny baby with a tiny mask on her face. She was struggling to breathe. My instincts told me to follow her, but my heart was still in that theatre room with Nikki. I had to leave her alone to be stitched up while I followed our newborn into the unknown.

Six days. That's how long Lottie was in neonatal ICU. And I visited every single day—juggling it all like I had done for months. Driving back and forth, checking on Nikki's recovery, keeping things normal for the kids, trying not to collapse.

That's when the emotional toll started leaking out in other ways.

Every single message from a customer through the Attentive chat sent me spiralling. I couldn't cope. I didn't want to hear about tracking numbers or hoodie delays. I was hanging on by a thread, and the business I'd built from the ground up suddenly felt like a monster I couldn't tame.

I was snapping. At strangers. At loved ones. I even commented on someone's post on my personal Facebook out of sheer rage and ended up going to their house to confront them. That wasn't me. I wasn't violent. But I was furious. Not at them—at everything.

Fortunately, no harm was done that day. But it was another warning sign I ignored.

Then came the part that nearly destroyed me: the resentment. The shame. The guilt. The raw truth.

I resented my own daughter.

I didn't want to admit it then, and even now it's hard to write. But I need to say it. Because I know other dads out there have felt it too—and they're just as afraid to speak about it.

I didn't feel that instant, overwhelming love I'd been told about. I was exhausted. Broken. I felt like Lottie had stolen Nikki from me. And she hadn't, of course. But I wouldn't let Nikki do anything. I wouldn't let her help. She offered—but I wouldn't allow it. Because that's how I controlled the chaos. I didn't let go.

So, I spiralled.

And I thought I was a bad dad for not feeling what I was "supposed" to feel.

Midwives would come in and ask how "mum and baby" were doing, and I'd smile and say "great," even though I was screaming inside.

No one ever asked how I was.

And that's when it hit me—men's mental health after becoming a parent is practically invisible.

There's this unspoken expectation that we just crack on. No space to pause. No time to fall apart. We're expected to be the strong one, the calm one, the rock. But what happens when the rock is crumbling?

Nobody checks in on the dad. There's no follow-up appointment. No mental health screening. No simple "Are you okay?"

And truthfully, I never spoke about how I was feeling—not properly. I bottled it all up, like so many of us do, until it spilled out in the worst way imaginable.

Because the truth is, emotionally—I was drowning.

Becoming a new dad hit me like a truck. Not just because of the sleepless nights or the fear around Lottie's health. It was the new pressure I'd never felt before. The weight of needing to provide. The constant worry of, Am I doing enough? Am I enough? Every day felt like a test I was failing.

I was suddenly responsible for keeping a tiny human alive, supporting Nikki through recovery, holding things together for the other kids, and somehow still being the "man of the house." And through all of that, I was silently judging myself. Every single day.

I felt like I was supposed to be grateful, glowing, overflowing with love—and instead, I felt… pressure. Fear. Guilt. This voice in my head telling me I wasn't cut out for this. That maybe I wasn't good enough to be someone's dad. That I wasn't present enough. Patient enough. Strong enough. Man enough.

I was trying to keep everyone happy. Everyone safe. Everyone fed and cared for and protected. But in doing that—I completely forgot about myself. I stopped checking in on how I was doing. I stopped treating myself with any kindness. I was burning out while smiling through it.

And the guilt was relentless. The guilt of feeling disconnected from Lottie. The guilt of snapping at customers. The guilt of not being able to be everything to everyone. I felt like I was failing my partner, my children, and my business all at once.

And behind all of that?

I was scared.

Scared I was going to mess everything up. Scared I wasn't enough for this family I'd fought so hard to build. Scared I'd lose them. Scared of the intrusive thoughts that kept creeping in. Scared that if I told someone how bad it had gotten, they'd think I was weak. Or worse—unfit to be a dad.

And I was feeling every single bit of it—raw.

Because before, I would've numbed this kind of pain with cocaine. That was my escape route. That was how I shut off the noise, buried the shame, quietened the overwhelm. But I was sober. I hadn't touched anything. And now, for the first time, I was feeling emotions in full force.

Big, overwhelming, unfiltered feelings—the kind I had spent years avoiding. The kind I'd sedated for so long, I didn't know how to survive without the buffer.

It was like being emotionally skinless. Everything hurt more. Everything cut deeper. And I had nowhere to run.

Then, on a day that should've felt like a celebration—Liverpool won the league again—I broke.

I kissed Lottie goodbye. Calmly left the house. Drove to a bridge that overlooked a busy A-road. I sat on the edge and prepared to jump.

I didn't want to die. I just didn't want to feel like this anymore. I didn't want to be a burden. I thought maybe, just maybe, everyone would be better off without me.

And then, a car came. Just a random car. Down a lane I'd never seen a car before, and I'd come to this place a lot to think in the past.

But it snapped me out of the trance.

I got back in my own. Drove home. Climbed into bed with Nikki. And I slept.

For 24 hours.

When I woke up, I was still here. Still broken. But still here.

That was the beginning of the turnaround.

I took time off. I paused Attentive. I went back to therapy. I upped my Venlafaxine. I let myself feel what I'd been running from.

And over time, that bond I thought would never come? It came. Quietly. Gently. And then all at once. Lottie became the glue I didn't know I needed.

In therapy, something else came up—something I hadn't expected.

I realised I was grieving again. Grieving someone who'd been gone for a while, but whose absence had suddenly become louder.

My grandad.

I was grieving the fact that he would never meet Lottie. That he'd never hold her, never tell her one of his daft stories, never give her one of those sideways smiles he used to give me when he was proud. And I know he would've loved her. I know he would've been so gentle with her. Playful. Warm. Funny.

And I found myself hoping—desperately hoping—that he would've been proud of me too. Of the man I'd become. Of the father I was trying to be. Of the way I showed up, even on the days when I had nothing left to give.

He never got to see me become a dad. But in those quiet moments, when I look at Lottie and feel the ache of missing him—I hope somehow, he knows. I hope he's watching. And I hope he's proud.

Eventually, I made the hardest but most freeing decision of my life: to close Attentive Apparel.

It wasn't failure. It was growth. It was me choosing peace over pressure. I realised that the brand gave me everything I needed to become who I am now. It led me to Nikki. To Grace. To Olly. To Lottie Bea.

To love. To purpose. To family.

So, if you're reading this, thinking you're broken or unworthy or failing just because you're struggling—please hear me:

Speak up. Even if all you can say is "I'm not okay." Speak up before the silence gets too loud. You are not a burden. You are allowed to feel. You are allowed to need help.

And if you can't speak… I hope you've got someone close enough to notice the silence.

Because you matter too.

FULL CIRCLE-
A LIFE RECLAIMED.

As I sit down to write the closing words of this book, I'm not the same man who began it. What started as a chaotic, confusing, and often painful existence has evolved into something far more meaningful—a life built on self-awareness, love, resilience, and authenticity. This book isn't just a collection of memories; it's a roadmap of my healing. A transformation. A reminder that even the most broken parts of us can become the foundation for something whole.

From the masked child who couldn't sit still or make sense of his own emotions, to the man brought to his knees by addiction, heartbreak, and mental illness—I've walked through fire. I've seen the worst of myself, but I've also uncovered the very best: the fighter, the father, the partner, the creator, the advocate. For every moment I doubted my worth, there's now a moment I can point to and say: I made it through that.

I'm sober. I'm self-aware. I'm medicated. I'm loved. I'm a dad. I'm engaged to the woman who sees every part of me and stays anyway. I've got three incredible kids—two I was lucky enough to be gifted, and one I helped create against all odds. I've built a brand that helps others like me feel seen and heard, and in doing that, I've found my voice too. This book started in darkness but ends in light.

I've made peace with my past. I understand my mind. And more than anything, I've learned that healing isn't a destination—it's a daily practice. Some days I still stumble. But now, I know how to get back up.

If there's one thing, I hope you take from these pages, it's this: whatever you've been through, no matter how lost or broken you feel, your story isn't over. There is still time. There is still hope. And there is still so much beauty waiting on the other side of pain. Thank you for walking this road with me.

Chris Maddocks

FOLLOW

chris.is.attentive

Made in the USA
Monee, IL
04 November 2026

67384605R00138